DAVIDSON COUNTY
MURDER & MAYHEM

CALEB SINK

THE
History
PRESS

Published by The History Press
Charleston, SC
www.historypress.com

First published 2024

Manufactured in the United States

ISBN 9781467157384

Library of Congress Control Number: 2024942021

CONTENTS

FOREWORD

When Caleb Sink first walked into the *Dispatch*, I immediately wondered why in the world I had agreed to let this soft-spoken, meek teen write for the newspaper. Journalists are not known for holding their tongues. They are usually somewhat abrasive, definitely aggressive and real go-getters. They have to be able to get the story, find and get sources to talk about sometimes extremely private matters for a news story. Real news writers stick their noses in where they are not wanted. I didn't see this quality in the well-mannered Caleb.

Before me stood a timid young man with incredible manners who seemed a bit shy. Caleb called me "ma'am" about fifteen times in five minutes, and I seemed to be doing all the talking. How was this bashful teenager going to be able to talk to people in his community, ask questions and turn that into an article?

My Lord, he did it, and he did it with maturity and writing skills far beyond some of the newspaper's contributors who had been writing for several years. There, I learned not to underestimate Caleb Sink. He was indeed a writer and a great storyteller. He continued to surprise me when I learned he was writing books about Davidson County's communities and people. From *Reeds Crossroads Then & Now*, a book about the small unincorporated community of Reeds, to *Inspiring Davidson County*, a collection of stories about little-known Davidson County residents making a positive impact on their community, Caleb has a way of bringing out the extraordinary in seemingly ordinary topics.

As a skilled researcher, his talents shine bright again in his sixth and newest book release, *Davidson County Murder & Mayhem*. He tells these dark stories with eloquence and respect, giving readers details that connect the past to the present. In chapter 1, we learn that the late Davidson County attorney Paul Glenn Stoner of the Brinkley Walser Stoner law firm is the grandson of Frank Harris, who was murdered in 1872 by his neighbor James Elliot, who swung a fence post at his skull. And readers will never eat a meal again in Roots on Main in Lexington without thinking about the gruesome death of Sarah Holland Springs in 1897, when the Main Street location was the March Hotel. Caleb lays out the facts of her shooting death in her bedroom as she and her husband, Adam Alexander Springs, the hotel's proprietor, slept.

In chapter 5, he shows us that the old adage "sticks and stone will break my bones, but words will never hurt me," is not true. Words hurt. They can even lead to murder, as in the true story of "Preventing an Assassination." We learn that Hugh Weaver, apparently so harmed by something Charles Spencer Davis had said about him, set out drunk and with a pistol to kill Davis "unless he took back something he said." Weaver did not win the shootout, however, and lost his life over words and bullets from Davis's pistol.

Caleb breathes new life into these stories from long ago, pulling from court records and newspaper clippings from across the state to tell these tales of some of Davidson County's most unscrupulous people and their victims. It is evident he has spent time researching these stories, and you won't regret the time you spend with this book. The only regret is the book coming to an end. It left me hoping for a *Murder & Mayhem, Part Two*. (Hint, hint, Caleb.)

—Jill Doss-Raines

ACKNOWLEDGEMENTS

This book would not have been possible without the help of numerous people and resources.

To the team at The History Press, I appreciate the opportunity to share these forgotten stories.

Most importantly, I am ever grateful to my family for their unwavering love and support.

A huge thank-you goes to my friend, Jill Doss-Raines, who has long informed our community through her work at the *Dispatch*. She took a chance on me as a teenager and gave me an opportunity to write for our local newspaper, and I'll always appreciate that. Her editing expertise made this work all the better. I also appreciate her agreeing to write the foreword.

The Davidson County Historical Museum team, especially director Caitlin Williams and registrar Stephen Harris, always assisted when I requested historical images, and I am grateful.

With court records of the nineteenth and early twentieth centuries being so sparse, the resources offered through the Davidson County Public Library, specifically digitized newspapers, are invaluable. Genealogist and historian Tonya Hensley at the Lexington Public Library History Room gladly assisted in any request I had for research.

I appreciate the staff of the State Archives of North Carolina for their prompt responses to records requests.

Lastly, I appreciate you, the reader, for taking the time out of your day to read these stories. Without you, this would be a mere waste of paper.

INTRODUCTION

History, despite its wrenching pain, cannot be unlived,
but if faced with courage, need not be lived again.
—Maya Angelou

In 2022, Davidson County, North Carolina, celebrated its two hundredth anniversary with theatrical performances, history tours and even virtual programs. These year-long festivities provided unique opportunities to honor our county's rich heritage and recognize those resourceful few who laid the foundation of our community.

As we honor the founding of our county and acknowledge the advancements it has made, one must note that there are stories our forefathers would prefer us not to uncover. Riddled throughout the past two centuries are stories as murky as the Yadkin River and hidden as deep as Boone's Cave. It is those types of stories precisely that *Davidson County Murder & Mayhem* seeks to highlight, not to glorify them but to prove our ancestors were far from perfect individuals.

When Davidson County came into being in 1822, it was named for a man who himself was a victim of a gruesome homicide. General William Lee Davidson, a citizen of Rowan County, was an officer in the Continental Army during the American Revolutionary War. On February 1, 1781, when he was not even forty years old, he was shot through his heart and fell dead on the banks of the Catawba River during the Battle of Cowan's Ford (the site of which now lies under Lake Norman). General Davidson's honorable

Opposite: The old Davidson County Courthouse, now the Davidson County Historical Museum, served as a functioning courthouse from 1858 to 1958. *North Carolina Postcards, North Carolina Collection, University of North Carolina at Chapel Hill.*

Above: The old Davidson County Jail was situated behind St. Stephen United Methodist Church in Lexington. The building has long since been torn down. *Davidson County Historical Museum.*

death permanently solidified his place as an American hero, but the county that bears his name has a past with oftentimes far less honor.

The *Greensboro Patriot* implied in 1895 that the Davidson County of that day was a place of lawlessness and misdeeds.

> *Davidson County is maintaining its reputation. Within the past week it reports another murder, a cutting array that will in all probability prove fatal to one of the participants, and a drowning. The law as administered there seems to have little terror for evil-doers.*

The *Patriot*'s view of Davidson County seems to have resonated across the state during that time. Earlier in 1895, when Baxter Shemwell awaited his

The second-floor courtroom of the old Davidson County Courthouse has undergone changes through the years but remains much the same. *Davidson County Historical Museum, H. Lee Waters Collection.*

trial for killing Dr. Robert Lee Payne, his attorneys motioned to transfer the case to a different county. Their reasons (which were many) were offered in an affidavit and reported in Raleigh's *News & Observer*. Among them was "that there have been seventeen trials in the county since the Surrender (1865) for murder with not a single conviction, all were acquitted save one who plead [*sic*] guilty of manslaughter." The affidavit stated further that the county held a "sentiment against capital punishment." Ultimately, the motion met denial, but these concerns remained throughout the trial.

Nearly two decades later in 1913, when Lee Ford was on trial for the murder of Lexington policeman Mel Garland, similar concerns arose. The prosecution presented affidavits signed by former sheriff P.J. Leonard and Reverend Henry Sheets, among others, stating "that 25 to 30 percent of the men whose names are in the jury box may be bought and sold in an election and that it would hardly be possible to keep all of these corrupt men out of the jury box." In this case, the judge found the concerns credible and ordered jurors be drawn from Forsyth County.

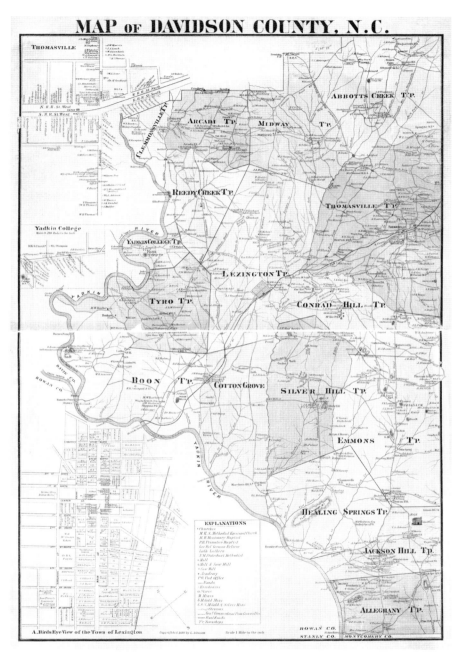

Nearly seven decades after Davidson County's inception, this 1890 map depicts each township, along with churches, businesses and homes. *Library of Congress, Geography and Map Division.*

Revolutionary War general William Lee Davidson was mortally wounded in battle in 1781. Davidson County bears his name. *North Carolina Department of Cultural Resources, North Carolina Highway Historical Marker Program.*

Looking through the lens of our present time to judge whether corruption existed in Davidson County in the past would be a difficult task. However, numerous accounts prove that some county citizens did indeed hold this sentiment. Perhaps by reading the many stories in this work, which span more than half a century, you may find an understanding of our history and, if you are so inclined, make a judgment on local justice in past times.

I hope that as you read *Davidson County Murder & Mayhem*, you will feel transported through time, as if you were a witness to the crime or a seeker of justice for each victim. In situations where we lack photographs, I ask that you use your imagination to envision the people and the places about which you will read. Who knows, perhaps you are related to one of the many characters, or maybe you live near the scene of a crime from long ago.

So, pour yourself a glass of tea, find a comfortable spot to read and settle in for a journey through the past.

1
NEIGHBORS KILLING ONE ANOTHER

Poet Robert Frost once wrote that "Good fences make good neighbors," and in Cotton Grove Township, long ago, a good fence could have prevented a murder among neighbors.

During the afternoon of Tuesday, October 1, 1872, thirty-four-year-old Jesse Franklin Harris went searching for stray sheep near his home. While passing the cornfields of his neighbor James Elliott, he discovered that his hogs had wandered into the cornfields and were being run down by Elliott's dogs. Harris quickly grabbed a stone and hit one of the dogs. Elliott, perhaps threateningly, told Harris to strike again, and when Harris kneeled as if to pick up another stone, Elliott grabbed a fence rail and hit Harris on his head with such force that it crushed his skull.

With Harris leaning against the fence, Elliott returned home to retrieve a bottle of camphor to rub on Harris while his mother-in-law, Rainey Owen, brought water from the spring to put on Harris's head. Other neighbors sent for Harris's wife and the doctor, though their presence would make no difference, as Harris had died almost instantaneously. Such was the end of Frank Harris's life and the beginning of the downfall of James Elliott.

At the time of Harris's death, he left behind a pregnant wife, Joicy Ann, whom he had married at the conclusion of the Civil War, along with two sons, James William Harris and Thomas Dow Harris. Meanwhile, as Elliott made his way to the county jail in Lexington, his wife, Elizabeth, remained uncertain of the future. Within less than a couple of months, James Elliott would face a jury of his peers.

The trial began at the fall term of superior court in early November 1872 at the Davidson County Courthouse. Despite the courthouse being only fourteen years old, its construction having been completed in 1858, it had gone through its fair share of wear and tear. Records indicate that the toll the Civil War had on the house of justice was substantial, and then, in November 1865, the building endured substantial fire damage. But by the time Judge John Martin Cloud arrived in Lexington seven years later to try James Elliott for his life, the building was in working order.

Judge Cloud, a bachelor in his early sixties, was a gentleman with a spotty reputation. Known by all accounts as an eccentric with a hatred of whistling, along with the noise of geese and chickens, Cloud's rough temperament was often the subject of criticism. An article in the *Charlotte Democrat* in April 1871 describes his judging in less than stellar terms:

> *He seems incapable of sitting quietly and dispassionately on the bench and hearing a case tried. He interferes with the examination of witnesses continually, sometimes leading them, and so persistently interfering with them, in a fidgety, passionate, and domineering style as to confuse utterly the current of testimony, and really show to the jury in every instance, just how much credence he thinks they ought to give to each witness and his testimony. Thus he really encroaches upon the province of the jury.*

The prosecution and the defense in the case were seasoned attorneys from across North Carolina; however, based on a newspaper account featured in the *Tri-Weekly Era* in Raleigh, we find that two stood out: James Madison Leach of Lexington for the defense and William Henry Bailey of Salisbury for the prosecution. Leach, in his late fifties, and Bailey, just over forty, were veterans of the Confederate Army with a reputation for their passion for the law, as demonstrated in the trial of James Elliott.

> *Before the trial had proceeded far it became evident that the contest was to be between Gen. Leach and Mr. Bailey, who is considered, where known, inferior in legal learning to no man in the State. General Leach defended his client with all his shrewdness and tact. After the jury had heard from him for four hours, and seemed worn out, still, when Mr. Bailey came to reply, all eyes turned to him, and never in my life (and I am a close observer) have I ever heard such an argument. His effort certainly was one of the best of his life, and stamps him as one of the first lawyers of the State. After the charge from his Honor, the jury retired and soon returned a verdict of*

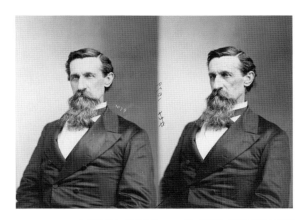

Top: James Madison Leach (1815–1891) was a renowned defense attorney and congressman. He was said to have lost only one murder trial in his career—his first. *Library of Congress, Brady-Handy Collection.*

Bottom: Thomas Settle Jr. (1831–1888) was an associate justice of the North Carolina Supreme Court and, later, a federal judge of the United States District Court. *Library of Congress, Brady-Handy Collection.*

"guilty." This case will not soon be forgotten, as no stone was left unturned on either side. No State has more real talent than old North Carolina.

James Elliott was found guilty and sentenced to death by hanging, which was scheduled to occur on December 20, 1872. He appealed to the Supreme Court of North Carolina, and the matter came before the court during the January term of 1873. Associate Justice Thomas Settle wrote the opinion of the court to grant Elliott's appeal for a new trial in superior court. Later in the year, Justice Settle also wrote the decision in the infamous *State v. Linkhaw* case, in which the supreme court overturned the guilty verdict of William Linkhaw of Robeson County for singing so terribly in church that he disturbed a religious congregation.

The justice, writing the court's opinion, stated that it was ultimately the testimony of Elliott's sister-in-law that won him his appeal. Elliott's attorneys had called Mrs. Beck, his wife's sister, to testify on his behalf. When the prosecution asked Mrs. Beck under cross-examination if she told Mrs. Ellen

Paul Glenn Stoner is the "Stoner" in the historic Brinkley Walser Stoner law firm in Lexington. *Author's collection.*

Lane on the day of the killing that Harris was "sitting up and she did not think he was hurt as bad as he pretended to be," she denied such a saying. The prosecution, refuting her testimony, called Mrs. Lane to the stand despite the defendant's objection. She testified that Mrs. Beck told her, "I sit him up against the fence and washed the blood off him. I do not think he is hurt very bad; he makes out like he is hurt a great deal worse than he is." It was this statement and Mrs. Lane's rebuttal of the defendant's witness that led to a new trial in Forsyth County. Justice Settle stated, "It may have so prejudiced the prisoner's case as to lead to his conviction."

Elliott's second trial began in neighboring Forsyth County in May 1873. He was convicted of manslaughter and sentenced to ten years in the North Carolina State Penitentiary in Raleigh—though how long he actually served is unknown. On October 18, 1885, when he was just forty-one years old, Elliott died and now rests in the Elliotts Grove Cemetery in Montgomery County. Elizabeth Elliott raised three children, James, Isaac and Nannie, in Eldorado Township in Montgomery County, where she died in 1921 at the age of eighty-seven.

On March 29, 1906, more than three decades after Frank Harris's murder, Harris's grandson Paul Glenn Stoner was born in Davidson County. He would go on to inherit the Harris homeplace in Southmont before selling it to furniture magnate Henry Link in 1964. Stoner would become one of the most respected attorneys in the county and the namesake of Stoner-Thomas School and the Brinkley Walser Stoner law firm in Lexington.

2
A BULLET FOR HIS BROTHER-IN-LAW

Often, it has been said that business and family should not mix, and no better example of this sentiment exists than the happenings of the Haden and Barber families in 1879.

Early in 1876, Ida Haden, the twenty-one-year-old daughter of wealthy Boone Township farmer James Wilson Haden, married a man who would change her family forever. That man, McCajah Wyatt "M.W." Barber, nearly twenty years Ida's senior, was a native of Pittsylvania County, Virginia, and made his way to Davidson County after spending a short time in Salisbury. After their marriage on April 25, 1876, officiated by esteemed Baptist evangelist Reverend Francis Marion Jordan, Barber and Haden settled in the western section of Davidson County. Here, Barber farmed and worked as a merchant in his own store.

Sometime after the marriage, Barber was at odds with his father-in-law in business dealings. This disagreement led to much animosity between Barber and his brother-in-law Robert Haden, and the two did not speak for an extended period. The specifics of the feud are unknown, but in March 1879, it arrived at a dramatic climax.

On the morning of Thursday, March 13, 1879, Barber was riding on horseback from Boone Township to Salisbury when he passed the home of Haden. The latter called for him, and bitter words flew between them. As Haden crossed the fence, he drew his fist and called Barber a liar while Barber spit in his face. When Haden grabbed the reins of Barber's horse,

Barber pulled his revolver and fired it. The ball entered Haden's left eye and passed into his brain, resulting in instantaneous death. Robert W. Haden was twenty-six years old.

Barber remained at the scene until he fled to the home of Dr. William Belvidere Meares to determine what he should do. Dr. Meares's colonial home, which he called Belvidere, sat near the Yadkin River in the Jersey area of the county on the lands that formerly belonged to the father of North Carolina governor John Willis Ellis. What advice Meares offered to Barber is unknown, but eventually, he went home, told his wife of the horrible affair—how he had killed her brother—kissed her and their young child and made his way to Lexington. A posse later confronted him and took him to jail, and James Haden vowed to have his son-in-law prosecuted to the fullest extent of the law.

In early May, the grand jury found a true bill of indictment against M.W. Barber for manslaughter, and the matter was set for trial later in the month.

When the trial began in mid-May 1879, the Honorable David Schenck of Lincoln County was the presiding judge. Schenck was a man respected across his district. An article in the *Charlotte Democrat* is quoted as saying, "His Honor is the working Judge, and it is remarkable with what rapidity he goes through a docket." He arrived in Lexington after holding court in Forsyth County and stayed at the stately March Hotel on Main Street while completing his docket.

As the trial of Barber was called by the judge, an impressive host of attorneys made their presence known. Prosecuting the case was the district solicitor, along with James Marshall McCorkle and William Henry Bailey, both of Salisbury. Defending Barber was James Madison Leach of Lexington, John Henry Welborn of Lexington, Cyrus Barksdale Watson of Winston and William B. Glenn of Winston (the towns of Winston and Salem did not merge until 1913). These men possessed much influence throughout the state as political leaders and orators and were well-versed in the legal system. In fact, just eight years earlier, McCorkle had served as legal counsel to Governor William Woods Holden during his impeachment trial before the North Carolina Senate. Despite adequate legal representation, Governor Holden became the first governor in the United States to be impeached and convicted in 1871 for his attempt to take a stand against the Ku Klux Klan. In 2011, 140 years later, the North Carolina Senate unanimously voted to pardon the governor.

Barber's trial, though dramatic, lasted only a short time, with the jury deliberating for only ten minutes. He was found not guilty of manslaughter

Left: Assisting in the defense of M.W. Barber was Cyrus Barksdale Watson (1845–1916), who previously studied law under Lexington attorney James Madison Leach. *From the* Biographical History of North Carolina, *vol. 4.*

Right: The grave of Robert W. Haden is located in the Jersey Baptist Church Cemetery off Linwood-Southmont Road. This centuries-old burial ground is in the National Register of Historic Places. *Find a Grave.*

in the killing of Haden. The *Winston Leader*'s report of the event makes it seem as though the audience was satisfied with the verdict:

> *There was an attempt to applaud when the jury rendered their verdict, which was quickly suppressed by His Honor.*

Barber remained in Boone Township, farming and selling merchandise for many years after the shooting, and by the late 1880s, he was a township justice of the peace. It seems he reconciled with his father-in-law at some point, as he officiated a wedding at the Haden home in 1888. Barber was also a key proponent in keeping crime rates down in the Jubilee community, where the justice often fined lawbreakers for fights. Eventually, he and his wife moved to Fulton Street in Salisbury, where they remained until their deaths.

Robert W. Haden, an unmarried man with no children, is remembered by only a small stone in the cemetery of Jersey Baptist Church in Linwood.

3
NO JUSTICE FOR MRS. SPRINGS

T hroughout history, there have been some mysteries that will undoubtedly never be solved. One of these head-scratchers abides on the streets of Lexington through an act of bloodshed that will never find justification. It's the cold-blooded murder of a fifty-one-year-old churchgoing wife and mother that remains a mystery to this very day.

In the wee hours of one summer morning in 1897, gunfire rang loudly through Lexington's March Hotel. Within minutes, Sarah Holland Springs, the wife of the hotel's proprietor, was dead—a bullet had passed through her left eye. Thus began the search for a killer that would never meet its end.

At some time past 3:00 a.m. on Wednesday, June 23, 1897, Mrs. Springs awoke to an intruder in her room in the hotel. As she raised herself in her bed and screamed, the intruder fired his pistol at her. Her husband, Adam Alexander Springs, who was said to be partially deaf, was awakened by the shot and leaped from the bed to catch the man. The killer quickly ran out of the room and into the hotel office, where he escaped through an open window.

As Mr. Springs sent for Drs. Joel and David Hill to tend to his wife, word quickly traveled throughout Lexington of the crime. The doctors could not help Mrs. Springs, and she died in bed without saying another word. At the time of Mrs. Springs's death, the March Hotel was operating at the former home of the late Dr. Robert Lee Payne Sr. on South Main Street. A new building was under construction at the corner of Main Street and West First Avenue. Just two years prior, Dr. Payne was shot down on the streets

These historical images of Adam Alexander Springs and Sarah Holland Springs appeared in the *Dispatch*'s special sesquicentennial edition. *From the* Dispatch, *October 6, 1972.*

of Lexington by infamous businessman Baxter Shemwell, who was later acquitted of the crime. Despite the acquittal, "ASSASSINATED" still appears on the doctor's gravestone.

Friends and neighbors arrived at the hotel after hearing of the tragedy and sought clues from Mr. Springs to help search for the murderer. He believed the bullet was intended for him, though he knew no enemies. The only description he could provide was that the man was white and of medium build.

John Kinney, deputy sheriff, telegraphed for bloodhounds and received word that William B. Hartsoe would bring them from Burlington on the first train. Despite his friends' teasing, Hartsoe had purchased the dogs in 1895 from a gentleman in Indiana for the sole purpose of catching criminals in North Carolina. Only a few months later, they were already in use in Gibsonville to catch an arsonist.

As the town awaited Hartsoe and his dogs, theories about the purpose of the crime began to swirl around town. Many believed that it stemmed from a string of attempted robberies that occurred during the night at the homes of businessmen George W. Mountcastle (located where the J. Smith Young YMCA now sits) and Thaddeus C. Ford (located near the present site of

First Baptist Church on West Third Avenue). At the Ford home, Caroline Ford heard her window rise, so she yelled. And then, when the window rose a second time, she said, "If you raise that window again, I will blow your brains out." When the prospective intruder lifted the window again, the elderly Mrs. Ford retrieved her gun, and the criminal left her home.

The bloodhounds from Burlington arrived by train around 3:00 p.m., approximately twelve hours after the crime was committed, and began tracking the suspect. By 4:00 p.m., the dogs and the armed men accompanying them had made their way to the edge of town while following a trail. When nightfall came, the dogs lost the scent in a dry field, and the searchers returned to town. As prospects of finding the suspect dimmed, Governor Daniel Russell, with a mere five months in office, offered the most substantial award possible, $400, for the arrest of the killer.

At 9:30 a.m. on June 24, just thirty hours after her murder, the funeral of Mrs. Springs was held at the First Baptist Church in Lexington. Many mourners gathered in the church (then located off South Main Street) to pay their respects in a service that featured five ministers and countless tears. A writer for the *Dispatch*, while memorializing Mrs. Springs, wrote,

In late 1897, the second March Hotel opened after the previous building had burned. The hotel operated in the home of the late Dr. Robert L. Payne before this building opened. *Davidson County Historical Museum.*

"She was a member of the Baptist church, and her Christian life, motherly kindness to all, gentle, unassuming disposition wrought an influence upon all who knew her well."

The brother of Mrs. Springs, John Holland, while searching for the killer on June 25, came upon the trail of a "suspicious character" spotted near the Welcome community. Mr. Holland followed the man to a location near Danville, Virginia. He described him as "a man of medium size, light hair, sharp face, slightly freckled, clean shaved, wearing dark blue clothes well worn, and a soft brown hat with narrow brim, and carried a book with names of post offices in Rockingham County, NC." But Mr. Holland lost the trail and returned to Lexington without his alleged suspect.

By mid-July 1897, the search for the killer had seemingly grown cold, that is until Mount Airy chief of police E.M. Taylor telegraphed for Mr. Springs: "Can you identify the person that murdered your wife? I have a man arrested answering description. Wire immediately." Mr. Springs replied, asking for a full description, and received one later in the day: "Height, five feet, ten inches; weight, one hundred and forty; sandy hair; light blue eyes; slightly freckled; first joint of little finger on right hand gone; scar over left eye; slightly bow-legged; age, twenty-two; name, Wiley Plesants Barlow. Wire what to do, quick."

Barlow's family story was one of interest and one that the law enforcement of that day knew about and the press publicized. In November 1891, in Davie County, Barlow's brother, John Barlow, had fought with young James Faircloth at a corn shucking. After being struck twelve times with a knife, Faircloth died, and John was found guilty at trial. Certainly knowing Barlow's family's negative reputation, Detective Seymour of the Pinkerton Detective

This postcard depicts Lexington's Main and Center Streets as they appeared in the years following Sarah Springs's murder. *North Carolina Postcards, North Carolina Collection, University of North Carolina at Chapel Hill.*

When the second March Hotel building burned to the ground, the building depicted here was built in its place and remains there. *North Carolina Postcards, North Carolina Collection, University of North Carolina at Chapel Hill.*

Agency and Mr. Holland left Lexington for Mount Airy the following morning to investigate. When they returned to Lexington, they were empty-handed, as they had determined Wiley Barlow was not their suspect. He later settled in the Clemmons area and died a widowed farmer in 1932.

With an unknown suspect and no clues, the Springs murder investigation became stagnant by the fall of 1897. Mr. Springs would ultimately leave Lexington and remarry before dying in 1925 in Norfolk, Virginia, taking to his grave any possibility of finding the killer.

The second March Hotel, which had been under construction at the time of Mrs. Springs's death, later burned, and a third hotel building was built at the site during the early twentieth century. Despite the hotel closing decades ago, that third building has stood the test of time and remains home to a restaurant, a specialty store and a tattoo parlor.

4
SUNDAY'S SERVICE LEADS TO A SHOOTOUT

If ever there was a man who affected Boone Township, Henry Clay Grubb was that man. When determining whether his impact was good or bad, well, the answer depends on who you ask.

Clay, as he was known to differentiate himself from his father, was born on November 22, 1870. His father, a twice-married farmer, having been widowed in 1862, married Clay's mother, Louisa Snider, in 1866. Her first husband, Private Alexander West, had died during the Civil War in 1864. Clay's parents raised him and his siblings in Boone Township, and here, he attended a primitive schoolhouse. At the age of eighteen, Clay started his own family when he married Emma Frances Davis. Born on February 22, 1875, the daughter of respected farmer William Thales Davis, Emma was just fourteen years old when she married Grubb at the Davis homeplace in the Horseshoe Neck Road area.

As he began his life as a husband and, shortly after, as a father, Grubb quickly displayed a keen business acumen. From farming and sawmilling to real estate and whiskey manufacturing—the shadiest of his businesses—Grubb accumulated large sums of money. But as Grubb built a reputation as a businessman, he also became known for his fiery temper. In fact, the earliest mention of Grubb in the newspaper told of a fight he engaged in with Alfred Snider, a man twenty years his senior, in 1894. Many incidents like this one would follow, Grubb's anger and fondness for strong drinks haunting him continually throughout his short life.

Henry Clay Grubb (1870–1913) was born in Boone Township, and it was here that he killed his brother-in-law. *From the* Salisbury Globe, *May 10, 1905.*

Reverend D.R. Myers had just opened the Bible at Piney Baptist Church, the predecessor of Churchland Baptist Church, around noon on Sunday, October 16, 1904. Suddenly, the holy scriptures were interrupted by the sound of gunfire. Three shots sounded, and someone said, "Davis is killed," as hundreds of congregants rushed from the sanctuary to the churchyard. There, they found Obediah "Obe" Lawrence Davis lying in a pool of blood and Henry Clay Grubb, his brother-in-law, holding the gun that killed him. Davis's death at just thirty-three years old was the climax of a long-fought battle between him and Grubb, which began, by all accounts, over money.

The shooting, no doubt, was the most tragic event up to that point in the history of Piney Baptist Church. Nearly seven decades prior, on May 17, 1837, the church had been organized with eleven members when they left Fork Baptist Church in Davie County to begin their own congregation. Both the Davis and Grubb families had taken active roles in the church, and these family names continue to hold influence in the congregation today. Despite the crime occurring long ago, it continues to make for interesting conversation among church members.

Grubb surrendered to Sheriff Thomas Samuel Franklin Dorsett in Lexington around 3:00 p.m. on Sunday. Immediately, according to news reports, Grubb said he had killed his wife's brother in self-defense: "Grubb says that just as he drove up near the church where a protracted meeting was going on, he saw Davis attempt to draw a pistol, and believing his own life to be in danger, he shot Davis to save himself." But just as immediate as his claims of self-defense were the stories of onlookers, who claimed Grubb committed cold-blooded murder. This further diminished the reputation of a troubled community, according to the *Dispatch*:

> *Boone township has been noted for its blockade whiskey and lawlessness for more than ten years. They have had numerous fights, shootings, house and barn burnings and the good people of that community have been afraid to open their mouths.…For a long time the good people of Boone township*

Top: The Grubb family lived in a mansion in Boone Township. In this 1908 photograph, daughters Zetta and Eula sit in the cart while brother Clay stands to the left and Theo stands with the pony. Daughter Beulah and mother, Emma, stand behind. *From* Homespun *(Summer 1982).*

Bottom: Pine Meeting House, situated in the Churchland community and organized in 1837, was the location of Obediah "Obe" Davis's murder. *From the* Salisbury Globe, *May 10, 1905.*

(and there are many good people in that section) have been afraid of these men and compelled to keep silent and permit the laws of the state and nation to be disregarded.

For many, the blame for the lawlessness in Boone Township lay at the feet of Grubb and Davis. Grubb's fight with Alfred Snider in 1894 was only the beginning of a string of indiscretions. In 1896, two alleged "regulators," W.W. Wilson and Wesley Smith, lost their barns to fire, and Wilson said he saw Davis strike the match. Davis ran, becoming an outlaw, and searches began. When Davis surrendered in November 1896, he was tried before Justice of the Peace M.W. Barber and found not guilty. The following years saw Grubb and Davis in shootings and fistfights, all while fending off trouble with the United States government over whiskey. In 1900, Grubb's large home and buildings were set on fire by an unknown person and burned to the ground. Two years later, perhaps to clean up his community, Grubb ran for sheriff and lost to the man whose jail he would eventually sit in, Sheriff Dorsett.

With no judge readily available to determine his bail, Grubb remained in jail awaiting a judge until early November. He then appeared with an army of attorneys at the Guilford County Courthouse before Judge O.H. Allen for a bail hearing. After hearing from various witnesses, Judge Allen denied Grubb bail and remanded him to the Davidson County Jail to await trial months later.

On Tuesday, February 28, 1905, a grand jury returned a true bill of indictment for murder against Grubb, and afterward, during his arraignment, Grubb made a plea of not guilty. But before the case could progress, Solicitor William Cicero Hammer motioned to have the case moved out of Davidson County, alleging it could not offer a fair trial.

Prosecuting attorneys presented more than twenty affidavits alleging that getting a fair trial in Davidson County would be impossible. The *Dispatch*'s editor described the prosecution's argument:

On the part of the State's contention that a fair trial could not be secured, affidavits were read showing that since the homicide, Grubb has not been confined nor treated like it is customary to treat prisoners charged with a crime, that he has contrary to custom, been allowed freedom in the corridor of the jail, allowed to receive and entertain visitors and friends regardless of numbers, that he has a stenographer and typewriter, a phone and bed installed for the express benefit of himself and friends; that he

kept quantities of spiritous liquors in the jail; that he has been allowed to bring in water and coal with the jail door unlocked and in the absence of the jailer; that he has been allowed to eat with the family of the jailer; that no conveniences or luxuries have been denied him; that Grubb has, through friends and agents, canvassed the county for the purpose of moulding public sentiment and to secure a jury that would not convict, regardless of the law or the evidence; that in view of this organized effort and corrupt practice and his wealth are such it would be impossible to get a jury to impartially try the case; that to try the case in Davidson would be a farce.

Grubb's attorneys' attempt to discredit the case of the prosecution for removal consisted of nearly thirty affidavits, including Grubb's own words. The attempt, however, was made in vain. Judge Henry Ravenscroft Bryan ruled the trial should occur in Rowan County. Henry Branson Varner, the editor of the *Dispatch* whom Grubb claimed was "an enemy of his," wrote an editorial in response to the judge's ruling that discouraged lawlessness in Davidson County:

The miscarriage of justice in the courts must stop. Davidson County has had enough and the time is ripe for the good people of the county to call a halt. Human life is entirely too cheap and there is nothing so badly needed

Opposite, left: William Cicero Hammer (1865–1930) was a newspaperman, congressman and attorney. Governor Charles Aycock appointed him solicitor in 1902. *From the* History of North Carolina, *vol. 6.*

Opposite, right: Henry Ravenscroft Bryan (1836–1919) of New Bern was a superior court judge for sixteen years. *From the* Salisbury Globe, *May 10, 1905.*

Right: Henry Branson Varner (1870–1925) purchased the *Dispatch* in 1896. He later served as the North Carolina commissioner of labor and as a chairman of the state prison board. *From the* News & Observer, *January 15, 1901.*

in this section as a strong and fixed determination on the part of every good citizen to see that all criminals are prosecuted, not persecuted, and that all murderers are brought to justice.

Grubb left the Davidson County Jail for Salisbury on Thursday, May 11, 1905, to face his murder charge. The location of his trial was one of historical significance. Built between 1855 and 1857, the Rowan County Courthouse on North Main Street was a stately setting. Its first superior court judge was John Willis Ellis, a native of Davidson County who would become governor in 1859. At the beginning of the Civil War, when President Abraham Lincoln requested troops from North Carolina, it was Ellis who replied, "I can be no party to this wicked violation of the laws of the country and to this war upon the liberties of a free people. You can get no troops from North Carolina." When Ellis died in 1861, he was buried less than ten miles from where the Grubb homeplace stood in Davidson County. More than four decades later, in Ellis's former courtroom, Clay Grubb learned his fate.

After Judge Bryan called this case at 2:00 p.m., three hours passed before a jury could be selected. Testimony began the following day, Friday, May 12, at 10:00 a.m., with the prosecution calling their first witness: Reverend John M. Bennett.

The Rowan County Courthouse was the scene of the trial of Henry Clay Grubb. *North Carolina Postcards, North Carolina Collection, University of North Carolina at Chapel Hill.*

Reverend Bennett had long served as a Baptist pastor in Davidson County, with many years spent at Piney Baptist, where he made his home. He testified that he had just finished praying when Reverend D.R. Myers began to read scripture and the shots sounded, according to the *Salisbury Evening Sun*'s transcript of his testimony:

> *It was the third Sabbath in October and I was sitting in my seat on the west side. The first I heard of the trouble was the shots. I heard somebody say, "Davis is shot." I hastened to him and saw him lying on the ground with his face down; I tried to talk to him, but he was too far gone. Someone said, "Let's move him out of the blood," which was then gathering about his mouth and nose. We moved him about two lengths of a man from the blood. His face was down and turned towards the school house. This was about 17 feet from where he was shot. As the man died, his sack coat was up over his shoulder, I saw a pistol in his pocket. I saw the defendant a short while and his manner was that of violence.*

Sam B. Crump was next to take the witness stand, as he had been with Davis in the churchyard when he sustained his mortal wounds.

The first thing I knew of the trouble was the shot. Mr. Grubb was at my right; I did not know that he was there, not having seen him since he left his team. Mr. Davis turned and Mr. Grubb stepped in front of me and fired twice. I think his first shot was behind my head. After the first shot Davis retreated, his hands being down by his side. He was going away from Mr. Grubb, who fired twice more. The dead man's back was then turned towards the defendant, who had his weapon down as if to pursue Mr. Davis. Little "Billy" Simerson said to Mr. Grubb, "You are in my custody," and the defendant replied, "Keep your hands off me, I don't know who are my friends in this crowd." This is the only thing I heard him say.

Witness after witness for the prosecution testified that Grubb had been the aggressor. Cleveland Leonard testified that after he heard the shots, he heard Grubb say, "Stand back, I don't know who my friends are here. Where is Lester Davis and Henry Charles, the s— of a b—." Similarly, Minnie Rice testified she heard Grubb say, "I have killed Obe Davis, where is Lester Davis and Henry Charles? I want to kill them and then I'll be satisfied." By Saturday evening, the state had rested its case, hoping it presented sufficient evidence to find Grubb guilty of murder. Fearing that a sermon would sway the verdict, Judge Bryan forbade the jurors from attending church services on Sunday.

The defense team, consisting of some of the most brilliant legal minds in North Carolina, began its case on Monday, May 15. Twenty-four-year-old Clarence Thompson, an employee of Grubb and a witness to the crime, was one of the first to take the stand. He alleged that Davis intended to kill Grubb:

About 8 weeks before the shooting Mr. Davis asked me to go to Salisbury with him. I told him I didn't care to go. He said, "I thought you were a friend of mine," and I told him I was. Then he said, "Clay Grubb has accused me of stealing old man George Green's money and he threatened to indict me. If he does, it will ruin me and he must be put out of the way. If I can't get somebody to do it, d—d if I can't do it myself." I told him I thought it was my duty to tell Mr. Grubb, and Davis said, "By G—, you'd better not." I did tell him soon to watch out for Davis said he'd kill him on first sight.

Thompson, among other defense witnesses, alleged that it was Davis who first grabbed for his pistol in the churchyard. He stated, "I saw Mr. Davis put his hand to his right hip pocket. A woman screamed and Grubb jumped from his buggy. He drew his pistol and shot. He shot twice more in rapid succession. Mr. Davis was still trying to get his gun and fell."

In a strange turn of events, Sheriff Dorsett took the witness stand for Grubb, his former political opponent. The sheriff testified despite allegedly being threatened by counsel for the prosecution with exposure at trial for "maintaining a negro woman and with offenses against morality." Just three years later, Dorsett's wife indeed divorced him due in part, no doubt, to his well-publicized affair with one Laura Hargrave. However, the alleged threat of exposure in 1905 did not prevent his valuable testimony for Grubb.

> *On Saturday, October 15, about 2 or 3 o'clock, Obe Davis came to my office in Lexington. He said he had heard that Clay Grubb tackled his brother, Lester Davis in Salisbury, and threatened to whip him. Obe said: "This thing has gone too far and I am going to Piney tomorrow to settle it." I told him not to do it, that it was near election and might defeat me which I would not have to happen for $500. He said, "No, it has gone too far and one of us must die." I said, "Obe, don't do that you would be hanged." He replied, "I'll do it in such a way as to make it appear self-defense." I begged him to let the friends of both settle it. He couldn't do that, he said, and then I said, "Obe, you'll try that and Clay will be too quick for you." He said, "I have been in shooting scrapes and have seen Clay in them. He gets excited and I don't. I'll go down there and shoot hell out of him, and if you hear that I get him, don't send for me. I'll come to Lexington and surrender."*

W.A. Hendrix, Kate Reid and J.T. Walser all testified that they heard Davis threaten Grubb's life. Walser even alleged Davis offered him money to kill Grubb, a sentiment Grubb would allude to in his own testimony.

On Tuesday, May 16, 1905, at 12:24 p.m., Clay Grubb took the witness stand. A reporter for the *Charlotte Daily Observer* described his appearance and demeanor: "He is a fine-looking fellow, wears good clothes, weighs about 190 pounds, and a perfect specimen of physical manhood. He is pleasant, looks none of the criminal, and is intelligent."

Thirty-four-year-old Grubb explained that he and Davis's trouble began in May 1904, when Grubb told people that Davis had stolen George Green's money. "I told him he couldn't expect me to keep such things as this a secret," said Grubb. Later, Grubb saw Davis at the Jackson Saloon on North Main Street in Salisbury. Davis asked him to "drop this matter," to which Grubb replied, "I'd rather live in peace and harmony." Then, around August, about two months before the shooting, Clarence Thompson told him he needed to watch out for Davis. "I knew Obe to be a dangerous and desperate man, the worst I ever knew," said Grubb before he described the fateful day in October:

> *I saw Crump and Obe Davis coming toward me. Obe threw his hand to his hip pocket and stepped back. He looked mad. Was about 6 feet away and seemed to be tugging at something. I heard my wife scream and I jumped from behind my buggy and shot. Davis then turned and still tugged at his gun. I shot again and saw him weaken. I did not know until I examined my pistol that I had shot three times.*

E.J. Justice, counsel for the prosecution, fiercely cross-examined the defendant, seeking to display a pattern of aggressive behavior by Grubb. He began by asking Grubb about slapping Jacob Feezor. "And you struck an old man 75 years old because he called you a liar?" asked Justice. "I don't think he is 75, not more than 65. This has been 5 years ago," responded Grubb. Justice continued to press the matter, and Grubb sought to explain: "Well, he is pretty vigorous yet. He had a terrific fight with his nephew a year ago." Later, Justice asked, "And you struck a lady of Rowan County, didn't you, Mr. Grubb?" Grubb's response appeared in the *Salisbury Evening Post*:

> *Yes sir, I slapped a woman. I'll tell you how that was. I was going home one day with a fellow and we stopped in at a store, just below Spencer, to get some beer. I didn't know that Mrs. Eagle, who kept the store, objected to being called "Aunt Betsy," a name I heard she got on the chain gang and said, "Aunt Betsy, you have a nice stock of goods here." She called me a s— of a b— and made at me with a cheese knife. I slapped her back.*

Wednesday, May 17, saw the final witnesses testify and the beginning of closing arguments. Perhaps the most important witness of the day for Grubb's case was W.D. Simmerson, Boone Township justice of the peace. He told of his attempt to arrest Grubb after the shooting: "I said, 'Clay, you have killed Obe Davis and I'll have to arrest you and take your pistol away from you.' He said, 'I hope you won't do that. Obe has tried to hire two or three men to kill me. I am sorry, but I had to kill the d—d rascal to keep him from getting me.'"

E.J. Justice began closing arguments for the prosecution, in many ways taking a somewhat spiritual approach to the jury, according to the *Charlotte Daily Observer*:

> *You may say Clay Grubb had no malice in his heart for Davis. I tell you the man who can see the death pallor of his victim, who shoots a man going to church, who sends his unprepared soul before its God, and in the presence of a minister say, "I killed him, damn him," is not speaking the words of a man who has any love for his enemy. He may be damned but if he is [shaking his fist vigorously at Grubb] you damned him. If he is a damned rascal, it's because you sent his soul to eternity before it was ready.*

Rowan County congressman Theodore Franklin Kluttz's argument for Grubb was described as "marvelous in its separation of the wheat from the chaff."

> *With all the money that the prosecution seems to have at its control, with all the array of learned and able counsel at its command, if there ever was this side of heaven or hell a man who would swear that Obe Davis was not a violent, dangerous, desperate man, they would have had him here as a witness. They did not bring him; they could not find him, not even in Boone Township, that benighted community, nor in Davidson County, that lawless section, as Mr. Justice would have you believe them.*

Attorneys from Lexington, Salisbury, Winston and beyond offered arguments for two days, including Senator Lee Slater Overman for the defense. The senator, known to his colleagues in Washington as the "grand old man of the South," would go on to serve in the Senate for nearly twenty-eight years. During World War I, he would serve as chairman of a committee in the Senate investigating German propaganda, which was given the moniker the Overman Committee. Grubb certainly benefited from Overman's presence on his defense team, and given his stature in the state, his argument surely weighed heavy on the jurors' minds when they convened at 7:15 p.m. on Friday, May 19.

Just past 7:30 a.m. on Saturday, Rowan County clerk of superior court J. Frank McCubbins asked juror M.L. Jackson, "How do you find?" Jackson responded, "Not guilty." Grubb was a free man for the first time since October 1904, and he left the courthouse to eat breakfast at a restaurant in Salisbury before going home. One would expect a not guilty verdict would

Lee Slater Overman (1854–1930) was a respected attorney and later a United States senator from 1903 to 1930. *Library of Congress.*

be the most dramatic of conclusions for Grubb's story, but that simply was not the case.

As Grubb and Clarence Thompson traveled from Churchland to Salisbury the following Monday, May 22, bullets began to fly. The men were in a buggy between the Grubb home and the Yadkin River when they became the victims of an ambush. Most injured was Thompson, who received more than ten wounds, while Grubb also sustained injuries all over his body. Grubb stated he saw two men, one being an enemy of his, Nat Crump, but he said the other was not recognizable. Upon Grubb's words, a search for Crump ensued far and wide, with a reward of $500 for his capture alive or $250 if he was brought in dead.

Crump escaped to the mountains of North Carolina, where he was ultimately captured and wounded in a small community known as Mud Cut. A summary of his confession—a startling one, at that—ran in the *Charlotte Daily Observer*:

> Crump says between the homicide and trial at Salisbury he was often told that if Grubb were acquitted it meant death to Crump's blockaded business, and that Mr. Grubb would largely be instrumental in having Crump declared an outlaw. He wanted to leave the county, but the men wanted him to stay and put Grubb out of the way, Lester Davis being chief planner....The half-dead desperado says he was offered no money to slay Grubb, but that he was goaded to it by fear that Grubb's liberty meant death to his license to defy the law. There is a show of sense and truth in this. Near South River, Crump has a sister-in-law, who remarked upon hearing of Grubb's acquittal, "Nat Crump will have to hit it," and when questioned she told substantially the story of Crump— that Grubb would have him outlawed and his business destroyed, because they were enemies.

The prisoner alleged that Lester Davis, Henry Charles and Dave Leonard had conspired with him to kill Grubb. Frank Hairston, he said, aided in the carefully planned shooting, though he escaped prosecution. When Crump was tried in court in August 1905, he received an eight-year sentence. Surprisingly, the grand jury did not return an indictment against Davis, Charles or Leonard.

Despite the bloodshed at Grubb's hand and the attempt on his life that followed, it would eventually be his own death, eight years later, that would make for the most dramatic of stories. Early in the morning on Saturday,

August 9, 1913, Henry Clay Grubb was shot and killed in his home by his wife, Emma.

The story goes that late in the evening of Friday, August 8, Grubb came into his home in Churchland intoxicated and continued to drink. At about ten o'clock that night, according to Grubb's son, Zeb, who was fifteen at the time, Grubb became violent with his wife. Though Zeb begged him to stop, Grubb beat Emma for some time. Grubb's daughters, Beulah and Edna, would testify that when their father decided to rest, he told his wife that when he awoke, "he was going to kill her, and all of the family, including Lester Davis, Mrs. Grubb's brother." When Grubb began to move as if he was waking, his wife fired three shots, killing him almost instantly. The coroner's jury determined that Mrs. Grubb killed her husband in self-defense, citing her broken nose, painful lacerations and bruising all over her body.

The roads leading to the Grubb home were filled with cars, buggies and wagons the following day as the funeral neared its beginning. The Piedmont Toll Bridge, which offered Rowan County folks passage over the Yadkin River, reported having more passengers in one day than it had ever had before. News reports suggested that anywhere from three to five thousand people across North Carolina gathered at the home to witness the service. Grubb, dressed in a black suit and a black bow tie, lay in the same room where he had met his end. His wife, still recovering from the severe beating he had inflicted on her, lay in a small building across the driveway; her bed had been moved to the door so she could watch the funeral. At her request, six members of the Salisbury Elks Lodge carried the casket to Mrs. Grubb so that she could view the body. "Tender hands raised the head of the injured woman that she might get a full view of the face of the dead husband,"

The Grubb building, now known as the Plaza in downtown Salisbury, was the brainchild of Henry Clay Grubb. *North Carolina Postcards, North Carolina Collection, University of North Carolina at Chapel Hill.*

wrote one reporter. "She took one long look at the corpse, closed her eyes and laid down. There was no outburst, though it must have been an awful moment for her."

In his death, Grubb left behind a complicated legacy. The *Dispatch*, perhaps, described it best: "Many told of his fine work of recent years toward the upbuilding of the community and his willingness to help every worthy cause. He was a big-hearted, good-natured man when not under the influence of liquor and numbered his friends in the county by the score."

Opposite: The Grubb Gazebo was previously located at the mansion of the family. After restoration, it was moved to its present location at the entrance of the Grubb Cemetery. *Author's collection.*

Right: Henry Clay Grubb and his family rest in the cemetery he created for his father in 1909. *Author's collection.*

He spent a large sum of money working on the roads in his community, built what was possibly the tallest building in North Carolina at the time in Salisbury (now known as the Plaza) and employed hundreds. Despite all of this, his downfall was alcohol—a downfall that not only ended the life of his brother-in-law but also led to the end of his own.

Emma Grubb lived more than three decades after the death of her husband. To add to the many tragic events of her life, in 1936, her son, Dr. Henry Clay Grubb Jr., died by suicide in her home while she was bringing in groceries. Just over ten years later, when she died at the age of seventy-one, her family buried her in the same plot as her husband at the Grubb Cemetery in Churchland. Some have speculated through the years that Mrs. Grubb was not her husband's killer. Instead, the rumor goes, she took the blame to spare another family member from prosecution. Those who could solve such a mystery have long since passed away, taking their answers to their graves in the family cemetery, which rests along Highway 150.

5
PREVENTING AN ASSASSINATION

R alph Waldo Emerson, the acclaimed poet, once wrote, "There is this to
be said in favor of drinking, that it takes the drunkard first out of society,
then out of the world." Though one could question the poet's logic, for
one Hampton Township citizen on an autumn day in 1906, drinking likely
led to his demise.

On Wednesday, November 21, 1906, thirty-two-year-old Charles Spencer
Davis, known as Spencer, killed Hugh Weaver near the Centenary Church on
Hampton Road. Weaver, who used various names, including Hugh Weaver,
Hugh Cline and Uriah Cline, was about sixty years old at the time of his
death. Davis told his story to the *Dispatch* shortly after the killing, claiming
self-defense.

Weaver came to my father's sawmill Wednesday and began hauling off
some slabs, saying that he would pay for them. I met Weaver at the gate
and forbade him moving the slabs. Weaver said he was not angry with me
but stated that he proposed to take the slabs and would pay the owner for
same. Later in the day, Weaver told the men around the sawmill that he was
going to kill me before night and displayed a loaded shell. I was hauling
lumber and had to pass Weaver's home. Weaver met me in the public road
in front of his home and opened fire on me, shooting twice. I pulled down
on him with my pistol but missed him. After his second shot, I fired twice
and both balls took effect. One struck Weaver in the knee and the other in
the abdomen. The wound inflicted by the latter proved fatal.

John Moyer was a Lexington mayor and justice of the peace. Though he had no formal legal education, one attorney remarked, "He had one of the most impartial judicial minds I have ever known." *From the* Dispatch, *May 6, 1903.*

The following Saturday, Davis and his attorneys appeared for a preliminary hearing before Lexington mayor John Moyer. Moyer had moved to Lexington from Rowan County as a young man in his teens and worked as a store clerk. Gradually, he taught himself the law while working in the register of deeds office and clerk of superior court's office. Moyer would eventually become a justice of the peace and serve as the mayor of Lexington for over a decade. In passing judgment on cases, revered attorney Emery Raper remarked about Moyer, "He possessed the legal mind to a degree that one rarely ever sees." Moyer's brilliant mind would certainly be on display at the Davis hearing when Sarah (the victim's wife) and neighbors Lewis Cornish, John Zimmerman and Milton Haley testified before him.

Sarah Cline stated that the trouble between Davis and Weaver had begun long before the fatal affair when, at some point, Davis knocked her husband down in a fight. She testified: "That about 1 o'clock on Wednesday the 21st, her husband, who had been drinking, stated that he would kill Davis unless he took back something he said," according to the *Dispatch*. She said her husband had taken his gun with him into the yard and shot a small bird before he situated himself in a cotton patch to wait for Davis to appear on the road. As she saw Davis heading down the road, she said she "went into the house that she might not see the trouble, and there went down on her knees and prayed that God would avert any trouble." Within a short time, she heard the gunfire that was exchanged and saw her husband approaching her home, "shot in the breast and in the back of the knee…the last wound being made as Cline started to the house."

Fifty-four-year-old farmer Lewis Cornish, in his testimony, stated that "he helped dress the body after night. It was still lying in the yard when he reached the house." In detail, Cornish described the extent of Weaver's wounds to his breast and knee.

John Zimmerman, who had to be tracked down by the sheriff while hunting to testify, was "five or six hundred yards off" when he heard the shots between the two men. With Davis carrying a pistol and Weaver a shotgun, Zimmerman could not say which he heard first. He insisted that when he heard the shots, he thought someone was hunting in the distance.

Milton Haley, a gentleman who was about the same age as Davis, proved to be the most lively and dramatic of witnesses. When asked if he lived in Hampton Township, he first said, "Yes," but then corrected himself. "In Hampton? Never! Not on your life! No Sir! Perish the thought!" Haley lived in Reedy Creek Township. He further stated that about one year prior, Davis had threatened to kill Weaver, saying, "Me and him can't live in one neighborhood together."

After hearing all the testimony, the attorneys for Davis motioned to have the matter transferred to superior court; they also motioned that the court grant their client's release on bail. Mayor Moyer granted the motion, with bail for Davis set at $2,000.

Judge Fred Moore of Asheville (the father of future North Carolina governor Daniel Moore) arrived in Lexington on Monday, March 4, 1907, to preside over the superior court and the case of the *State v. Davis*. With a full docket—and the Davis matter among the most serious of offenses—most eyes focused on another case of less importance. On Tuesday, millionaire Frank Henry Fleer, the founder of the Frank H. Fleer Corporation and the man behind Dubble Bubble bubble gum, appeared in court. He was charged with hunting without a license on his land in Thomasville and eventually settled the matter for twenty-five dollars. Despite his trouble with the law, Fleer spent much of his time in Davidson County and died at his home in Thomasville in 1921.

When Spencer Davis's case eventually made it to trial, he pleaded not guilty by reason of self-defense. The matter met with a swift resolution, and Davis's judgment was not guilty. He lived another fifty years, dying at the age of eighty-three, and was buried in the Clemmons First Baptist Church Cemetery.

6
SLAYER PAYS WITH HIS LIFE

Across the world, through the portals of history, the biblical principle of "an eye for an eye," found in the book of Exodus, has been a recurring theme. In many instances, this idea of proportional punishment has been debated and continues to be. But over a century ago, here in Davidson County, a form of swift justice was carried out that exemplified "an eye for an eye."

Captain William D. Hughes, a foreman for the Southern Railway (the predecessor of Norfolk Southern Railway), was shot down along railroad tracks near Thomasville on February 6, 1906. Moments later, in an act of retribution, his assassin, twenty-seven-year-old W. Avery Darr, met his death a short distance away.

It was between 4:00 p.m. and 5:00 p.m. that Tuesday afternoon when Hughes and his crew were working some three miles from Thomasville and saw three men approaching them. Walking from High Point to Thomasville were Avery Darr, Clarence Spencer and Charles Lookabill. The men asked Hughes if they could ride the railway handcar into Thomasville. One account of Hughes's response says that he denied the men use of the handcar, though another says he would not allow Darr to ride because he was drunk. Either way, Darr's friends' attempts to calm him were futile, and he began to curse Hughes. After walking away for a time, Darr returned with his companions and offered Hughes an apology, at which time, Hughes asked him to leave. Darr refused to leave, and Hughes warned him that "he would take a pick handle to him if he didn't leave." Darr began to curse Hughes again and then shot him in the shoulder with a .38 Colt revolver, offering no warning. After he was shot, Hughes began to try to retrieve Darr's gun and took a second bullet to his back, with a third shot "going wild." "Come here, boys," were Hughes's last words as he called for his workers, having sustained two wounds. Within twenty minutes of the shots, he was dead at less than forty years old.

Darr, after he was struck in the head with a railroad pick by an unnamed worker, dropped his revolver and took off running toward nearby woods. One of Hughes's workers, Will Barnhardt, quickly grabbed Darr's gun. When Darr was fifty yards away, Barnhardt fired, striking him in the back below his shoulder. Darr's friends, who alleged the shooting occurred after he fell to the ground, said Darr called for them, saying, "O Lordy, Charles [Lookabill], come here and help me." Lookabill claimed Barnhardt threatened to kill him if he went to Darr's aid, though Barnhardt stated that his victim had met his end instantaneously. In a twist of fate, four years later, a train that was traveling tracks in Thomasville struck Darr's friend Charles "Chad" Lookabill and killed him.

When word of the killings spread across the community, overall sadness ensued. The scene was described in the *Dispatch* in the most dramatic of ways.

Those who witnessed it say that they never saw nor do they expect to see any sadder scene than that which took place at the Hughes home when it was known that the father and husband was dead and when the body was taken to the house. The little ones climbed over the body and tried to make the dead tongue speak to them. Men cried like children and in all Thomasville it might be said that there was hardly a dry eye. The whole affair is one of the saddest, most uncalled for, as well as one of the most terrible happenings that ever took place in Davidson.

The bodies of Hughes and Barnhardt were taken to Thomasville. This postcard, circa 1905–15, depicts Salem Street. *North Carolina Postcards, North Carolina Collection, University of North Carolina at Chapel Hill.*

Thomas Samuel Franklin Dorsett
(1862–1916) was the sheriff of
Davidson County from 1898 to 1906.
From the Dispatch, *February 14, 1906.*

Sheriff Thomas Samuel Franklin Dorsett arrived in Thomasville the night of the shooting to investigate but left the following morning to return to Lexington—without arresting the only surviving shooter. A writer for the *Dispatch* reporting on the incident wrote, "Will Barnhardt is at Thomasville and has not yet been arrested, for he seems to have many friends, and public sentiment in Thomasville appears to be with him. Leading men there told the sheriff that they would go on his bond for heavy amounts and that he would be present when the trial comes off."

The preliminary trial of Will Barnhardt for the murder of Darr began on Thursday, February 8, before John Keen, justice of the peace at Thomasville, and Dr. Charles A. Julian, the county coroner. Barnhardt's trial was held before two of the most esteemed men in the town. Keen had a background in milling and tobacco before he moved to Thomasville between the late 1880s and early 1890s. Here, he served as mayor for a time, and folks described him as "one of the best justices in the county." Dr. Julian arrived in Thomasville around the same time as Keen. And here, he married the granddaughter of the founder of the town, John W. Thomas. The young doctor established a successful medical practice and served many years as the county coroner.

In his trial, Barnhardt's story of self-defense met with corroboration from his coworkers who were working on the railway that day. The verdict was a resounding not guilty by reason of self-defense.

Barnhardt left the county for Greensboro after the verdict but returned to Thomasville to board a train to an unknown location the following Saturday. A *Dispatch* writer reported, "We hear that Barnhardt was 'put in good shape' by his friends in Thomasville," but what became of the gentleman is unknown.

Martitia Hughes, William Hughes's wife, moved their many children to Worthville Township in Randolph County, where she raised them alone. By the 1910 census, Epsie, their eldest daughter, was no longer attending school and instead worked in a cotton mill to help support the family. Some of

William A. "Avery" Darr's grave is located in the Pilgrim Reformed Church Cemetery, where his parents also rest. *Find a Grave.*

the family later returned to Davidson County, and Mrs. Hughes died at the home of her daughter in Lexington in 1946.

Darr's wife, Jeanette Florence "Nettie" Darr, whom he married in 1904, remarried in 1913 and lived in Lexington until she died in 1984. She lived to be one hundred years old, with nearly eight decades passing after her first husband's untimely and unnecessary death.

7
FAILED TO MAKE A CASE

They say that the truth will set you free, and for three railroad workers long ago, their version of the truth, along with capable attorneys, indeed set them free.

Some time during the night of Saturday, November 23, 1912, Rassie Farris Butler, an eighteen-year-old man who was reared in Randolph County, was critically shot. His acquaintance J.A. Michael of Southmont was also injured. Together, the men had carried liquor to a construction camp along the Carolina and Yadkin River Railroad in Healing Springs, which led to a shootout. Within a short time, Dr. Arthur A. York of Southmont transported young Butler to St. Leo's Hospital in Greensboro for treatment, where he died the following Monday.

By Wednesday, an article retelling the events that had transpired in Healing Springs graced the front page of the *Dispatch*, offering an account of what may have occurred:

> *According to a version of the affair given by young Butler before his death, he went to the camp with Michael about 9 o'clock Sunday morning instead of at 2 o'clock. The negroes attempted to rob the two white men, whereupon Michael and Butler opened fire, the negroes returning with shotguns. Two of the negroes were shot, but how seriously has not been established. It was said that officers of Rowan and Davidson were in search of the negroes, but no reports were received last night from the searching party.*

St. Leo's Hospital, Greensboro, N. C.

REWARD!

A reward of Twenty-Five ($25) Dollars will be paid to the person or persons delivering to the Sheriff of Davidson County, or causing the arrest of, L. C. Harris for being implicated in the murder of Rassie Butler at the camp of the Carolina & Yadkin River Railroad, between Denton and High Rock, Davidson County, N. C., on the night of November 23rd. Harris was boss of the construction work for Lane & Co. He is about 5 feet, 6 inches high, with dark sandy hair, blue eyes, red face, smooth shaven, slim build and a little bow-legged, has well-dressed appearance: is about 25 years old and weighs about 125 or 130 pounds. The Lane Company has work going on at Norwood, Salisbury, and Baltimore.

W. V. BUTLER,

SOUTHMONT, N. C.

Above: A critically injured Rassie Butler was taken to St. Leo's Hospital in Greensboro. This Catholic hospital began its work in 1906, operated by the Sisters of Charity. *North Carolina Postcards, North Carolina Collection, University of North Carolina at Chapel Hill.*

Left: After the death of his brother, Wiley Butler offered a reward of twenty-five dollars for the arrest of his brother's alleged killer. *From the Dispatch, December 11, 1912.*

Later in the article, however, a very different version of events appeared:

It is rumored that no negroes took part in the shooting; that it was done by the white bosses at the camp who objected to Michael's liquor selling.

In the days following the death of Butler, his thirty-seven-year-old brother, Wiley Butler, began his own investigation into his youngest brother's murder. By December 4, he had a suspect: L.C. Harris, the paymaster for railroad contractors Lane Brothers. The bereaved brother ran a reward advertisement in the *Dispatch*, writing, "A reward of twenty-five dollars ($25) will be paid to the person or persons delivering to the Sheriff of Davidson County, or causing the arrest of L.C. Harris for being implicated in the murder of Rassie Butler." Another week passed with Harris still on the lam, but many believed he remained in the county.

The impression is that he has gone to his people to arrange for bond and get ready for his defense. The young man, it is learned, denies that he shot at Butler, though he admits he shot Michael. He claims that he did not shoot at Michael until Michael had fired at him three times with an automatic pistol. Butler, he claims, was shot by a negro. On Monday following the shooting it was reported that a mob composed of friends of Butler and Michael had been formed and was coming to lynch him and he left.

As the year 1913 began, the search for one fugitive expanded to include three fugitives as Governor William W. Kitchin issued a $100 reward each for the capture of L.C. Harris, Ike Ellis (the commissary clerk for Lane Brothers) and C.C. Duncan (a foreman for Lane Brothers). All three of these men were wanted for the murder of Butler and wounding of Michael.

After months of searching, February 1913 brought a conclusion to the murder of Rassie Butler. Harris, Ellis and Duncan were all arrested, Ellis and Duncan were retrieved from Atlanta, Georgia, by Davidson County deputy sheriff Fletcher Caudle. A preliminary hearing was set for the defendants on Saturday, February 8, at 10:00 a.m. before Lexington mayor John Moyer.

The defendants arrived in court with four attorneys, two from Lexington and two from Atlanta, along with a carefully crafted story. Ultimately, their plan to blame an unnamed "negro" for the murder of Butler proved successful, and Harris, Ellis and Duncan were found not guilty by John Moyer, known as "Squire Moyer."

Squire Moyer was clearly right in his verdict. The state failed utterly to make out a case, and it failed, it is said, because witnesses refused to go on the stand and tell what they knew. Three men who call themselves law-abiding citizens, said to have been eyewitnesses to a great many of the things that happened on the night of the murder, refused to tell a thing about it….Several other suffered severe lapses of memory and could call to mind none of the details of that memorable night.

In Harris's testimony, he relayed much the same story as he had previously told, stating, "[Harris] tripped and fell and dropped his gun" and that "the negro seized it and immediately shot Butler." Harris then "recovered his gun and shot at Michael who was standing behind his horse, pumping lead at him with an automatic pistol."

Another witness, quoted only as a "good citizen," put to bed any belief that Harris acted as a good Samaritan to Butler after he sustained his bullet wounds. Instead, his actions were described as that of a "savage."

A good citizen was drawn to the scene by the commotion and was present when Butler was found….This witness had taken Harris' gun from him and Harris begged for its return, saying that he was going to shoot Butler's heart out. Again, after Butler had been carried to the camp and was in a very serious condition, Harris called him a liar and threatened to drag him from his bed and "stomp the life out of him."

Nevertheless, the three defendants were released and free to return to their homes, leaving no one accountable for the death of a young man in the prime of his life. A writer for the *Dispatch*, while relaying the verdict, cited a failure of law enforcement to discharge their duties.

Nobody seemed to consider it his business to find out how Rassie Butler met his death. The justice of the peace who resides in the vicinity of the camp issued no warrants and there were no arrests. Until relatives of the dead man took the matter up and started an investigation little was done. If the case had been investigated thoroughly on Sunday following the shooting, the matter might have been cleared up and the guilty party or parties would now be behind bars….While it is the general belief that Butler was killed by one of the three men, no one was surprised at the outcome of the hearing.

Young Rassie Farris Butler was buried in Fairview Cemetery in the Liberty community of Randolph County. Whatever became of Harris, Ellis and Duncan is lost to history.

8
SHOT DOWN IN COLD BLOOD

In February 1946, former Lexington resident Lee Ford died at a hospital in Raleigh after being a patient for over eighteen years. Before his hospitalization for mental illness, Ford had been an inmate at the state prison since 1913 for killing a man in cold blood. His victim, Jesse "Mel" Garland, a textile worker and part-time policeman, left behind a widow and three young children when Ford gunned him down on Depot Street in Lexington.

On the afternoon of Friday, April 4, 1913, Garland was returning to work at the Siceloff Manufacturing Company after having lunch at his home. As he approached the business, Ford stepped out from behind the fence he was hiding behind, raised a shotgun and fired at Garland. Garland turned around to face Ford, grabbed his gun and dropped it as the second shot rang out. As Ford fired the third shot, Garland fell and died. Forty-one-year-old Ford approached his victim, slipped his gun under his arm and walked away. Within moments, deputy sheriff Fletcher Caudle, who had been at the Southern Railway Depot a short distance away, arrested Ford and took him to the county jail.

Ford's motive for the crime stemmed from his belief that Garland "had slandered him while he [Ford] was living in Texas." Ford so strongly believed in Garland's indiscretions toward him that he visited Lexington attorney Emery Raper to discuss "if there was some way in which he could get even with Garland." His method of getting even would ultimately lead him to plan Garland's death. Ford's father, Frank Ford, whom he lived with at the

Opposite, top: Siceloff Manufacturing Company, a Lexington manufacturer of overalls and work pants, was founded in 1908. Mel Garland worked at the company at the time of his tragic death. *Davidson County Historical Museum, H. Lee Waters Photography Collection.*

Opposite, bottom: Deputy Sheriff Fletcher Caudle was at the Lexington Depot and heard the shots that killed Mel Garland a short distance away. *The Winston-Salem Southbound Railway.*

Above: This undated postcard shows ladies gathering at the Lexington Depot. Garland's murder occurred somewhere near this location. *North Carolina Postcards, North Carolina Collection, University of North Carolina at Chapel Hill.*

time, stated that when his son came home for lunch that day in April, "he prepared a change of clothing and laid out his Sunday suit on his bed" before grabbing his gun and returning to work. The *Dispatch* reported that "after the killing, he [Ford] asked the officers to accompany him by his room, and there he put on the clean clothes he had laid out."

Ford appeared for his bail hearing before Judge Percy Vann Critcher of the recorder's court on April 15. Lexington attorney Lister Martin, in his longtime *Dispatch* column "Around Court Square," wrote of Critcher: "I have always understood that it is a sinful thing to be envious toward another. If so, I have been the chief sinner in this field for more than forty years—at least I have been sinning ever since I have known P.V. Critcher—for I have always envied him in his disposition—I have always wanted to be like him—to have his disposition and his generosity—and to possess his patience and tolerance toward people and things." But Judge Critcher was not generous toward Ford when he denied his bail and remanded him to jail.

> *Ford made a good appearance. He was neatly dressed, and except for a few moments when he was brought into the courtroom, he was calm and collected. He did not look around him but sat with downcast eyes, speaking only once or twice to his attorneys. Mrs. Ford was in court with a brother and other relatives. She is a very attractive little woman, and the hearts of the whole crowd went out to her. Her face showed traces of much suffering and many sleepless nights, and tears streamed down her cheeks as she sat behind her husband and listened to the lawyers.*

By late July 1913, just days away from the beginning of his trial, Ford, who had now been in jail for more than three months, appeared to onlookers to be unconcerned about his fate.

> *Mr. Ford, according to all reports, takes the matter very calmly and does not seem to be worried about the outcome, one way or the other. He steadfastly maintains that he had a perfect right to kill Garland and that it will appear when the case comes to trial. The idea that he may not be released never seems to have entered his mind. From the beginning, he has shown a strange lack of interest in the case. One of his attorneys is authority for the statement that Ford has not taken the slightest interest in his lawyers....He has not asked for his lawyers at all. This is taken by many to show insanity.*

On Wednesday, July 30, Ford was arraigned and pleaded not guilty to the indictment for murder. The prosecution, alleging corruption in Davidson County, motioned that a jury should appear from another county. They presented multiple affidavits alluding to corruption among the local citizens. The defense, while disputing such claims, agreed to have the jury drawn from Forsyth County, with the trial beginning the following Monday.

The jurors selected from Forsyth County arrived by train at 1:51 p.m. on Monday, August 4, and within a short time, twelve men took up the task of deciding if Lee Ford was insane.

Attorney Raper, who, years later, would die in the very courtroom where this case unfolded, was the first witness to take the stand concerning Ford's intentions to "get even" with Garland. Raper, a man small in stature, though

Top: Lee Ford found himself behind bars in the Davidson County Jail after killing Jesse "Mel" Garland. *Davidson County Historical Museum.*

Bottom: Main Street in Lexington; the Davidson County Courthouse can be seen in the distance of this circa-1906 postcard. *North Carolina Postcards, North Carolina Collection, University of North Carolina at Chapel Hill.*

a shrewd attorney, was normally the one questioning witnesses, not testifying himself. In fact, once, after Raper embarrassed a witness while questioning him on the stand, the witness "caught him outside near the town pump and dunked him bodily in the watering trough." While testifying, Raper stated that he "believed at that time that Ford was mentally unbalanced." Later, Ford's wife, Daisy, testified, "citing many instances that indicated an unbalanced mind. She told a good story, made a fine witness for her husband, and stood up well under cross-examination." The following day, numerous other witnesses testified, including Dr. Issac Taylor, the founder of the Broadoaks Sanatorium in Morganton, a facility that accepted patients with mental illnesses along with those who abused drugs or alcohol. Both Dr. Taylor and Dr. Eli Buchanan, a respected Lexington physician, testified to their belief that Ford was insane.

When the prosecution began their case to prove that Ford was indeed sane and capable of going on trial for murder, they attempted to discredit the witnesses and were successful. After eighteen hours of deliberation, the jury declared Lee Ford sane.

> *The suspense, especially on Ford's devoted little wife and other members of his family, had been terrible. When the jury filed in with its verdict, he paid no attention to it. The big crowd that filled the courtroom to the door held its breath, and there was a tense stillness in the room. Ford's little boy was in his arms, and he seemed to see nothing and hear nothing but the child. Mrs. Ford broke down when the verdict was read and cried piteously for half an hour or longer, but Ford never paid the slightest attention to it. His face was almost entirely expressionless and, apparently, he was the most unconcerned person in the courtroom.*

In November 1913, Ford pleaded guilty to second-degree murder and asked for the lightest possible sentence. Judge Thomas Shaw sentenced him to thirty years in prison, the maximum possible sentence. The *Dispatch* described his reasoning:

> *Judge Shaw said that while it was a terrible thing to take away hope from the human breast, there are times when it is necessary. He said that the defendant claimed that at the time he shot and killed Policeman J.M. Garland last spring, he was suffering from paranoia and was not responsible for his acts. There is no hope for the victim of paranoia and he can never be trusted with his family again. The paranoiac always turns against those who are near and dear to him, and it would never be safe for Ford to be with his wife and children again.*

The reporter also described how Ford's response to his sentence was one utterly lacking emotion:

> *Ford took the passing of sentence upon him with the same stoical calm that has characterized his every action since he killed Garland. The expression of his face never changed a particle, and he looked curiously, almost indifferently, at his faithful little wife, who was crying like her heart would break. He did not seem to realize what was happening to him.*

Left: Emery Elisha Raper (1863–1931), an esteemed Lexington attorney, died in the Davidson County Courthouse during a trial involving the Southern Railway Company. *Centennial History of Davidson County.*

Right: Lee Ford died in Raleigh in 1946 and returned to Davidson County to be buried in the Lexington City Cemetery. *Find a Grave.*

Ford left Lexington by train for the state prison in Raleigh just two days after his sentencing. "He showed no trace of emotion and carried himself with as much dignity as if he had been starting off to visit a friend, or take a pleasure trip," according to the *Dispatch*. When he returned to Lexington nearly thirty-three years later, it was only to be buried in the city cemetery.

Records suggest that Ford was moved from the state penitentiary to the state mental hospital in January 1928. What ultimately led to his removal to the hospital is unknown, but he lived out his life here, meeting his death in 1946 due to coronary thrombosis.

Alone, Daisy Thomason Ford raised three successful children: Elizabeth, Franklin and Robert. Elizabeth, known later in life affectionately as "Aunt Libby," was a bookkeeper and was described as a "guardian angel" to her family. Frank moved to Eden, North Carolina, and ultimately retired from a plumbing company after fifty years. Robert, who was only a year old when his father went to prison, retired as a major in the United States Army.

The three children of the slain man, Mel Garland, were placed in the care of the Thomasville Baptist Orphanage, now known as the Baptist Children's Homes of North Carolina. In 1921, Garland's eldest son, Melvin, was struck in the head and found on the streets of Norfolk, Virginia, where he had been working. Weeks later, he died at a Norfolk hospital at just eighteen years old. By 1930, seventeen years after her husband's killing on Lexington's streets,

Bessie Garland had moved to Winston-Salem and was able to retrieve her other children from the orphanage. She lived another two decades, and her children Grace and George lived long lives in Winston-Salem.

Today, the Depot District in Lexington is beginning to develop through efforts of both the city government and private businesses, and landscapes are changing as the area becomes a destination. An amphitheater, a farmers' market, a gym and breweries make up the district, which has gradually become more modern. Nothing would suggest that more than a century ago, in that very area, two families were changed forever because of one man's actions.

9

WIFE'S LOVER FINDS DEMISE

Boys, don't ever have good friends; you can trust them too far." Such were the words of J. Graham Hege moments after killing J. Frank Deaderick, a man he described as "the best friend he had in the world," in March 1918.

One might wonder what would lead a man to kill his best friend, and in this story, the answer is simple. For Hege, the bitterness that ended his great friendship and Deaderick's life resulted from a yearslong extramarital affair. That affair and the resulting crime would change the landscape of Lexington's social and business community.

John Graham Hege was born in 1887 in Lexington, his family having deep roots in Davidson County. His father, Henry, moved to Lexington as a young man to establish a marble business near present-day Marble Alley. Young Graham Hege married Edith Pugh in 1906 and began a career in upholstery. By 1916, Hege was an officer in the Southern Upholstery Company on North Main Street, which he helped found.

John Franklin Deaderick was a newcomer to Lexington. He was born in 1878 in Knoxville, Tennessee, to Thomas Oakley Deaderick, a university professor, and Josephine Heiskell Deaderick. On both sides of his family tree were men of prominence, politicians, business leaders and the like. Deaderick married Alma Rodgers and moved to Lexington, where he was elected the first cashier of the Commercial and Savings Bank in 1907, when the bank was established on Main Street.

Above: This photograph shows Main Street looking north as it appeared sometime between 1915 and 1930. *North Carolina Postcards, North Carolina Collection, University of North Carolina at Chapel Hill.*

Opposite, top: From the Commercial and Savings Bank's inception in 1907 until J. Frank Deaderick died in 1918, Deaderick served as the cashier of the bank. This advertisement for the bank is dated September 11, 1907. *The North State.*

Opposite, bottom: The Hege and Deaderick families settled in rented homes across the street from the Lexington Graded School, later known as Robbins School. This site currently houses the Robbins Recreation Center. *North Carolina Postcards, North Carolina Collection, University of North Carolina at Chapel Hill.*

How the two friends first came to meet is unknown; however, sometime after meeting, they became neighbors, both renting homes from Mrs. Banks Radcliffe. Hege selected a home on Hargrave Street, across from the Lexington Graded School (later known as Robbins School, named after Lexington attorney Frank C. Robbins), and Deaderick moved into a residence on Fifth Avenue. The two regularly visited one another at their homes and played cards together with their wives. That is, of course, until things began to go awry for the men on Monday, February 4, 1918.

It was on that Monday in early February that Hege first began to suspect there was a relationship between his wife and Deaderick. He had returned home to find Deaderick and his wife, Edith, talking along the fence line. When he confronted the two about his suspicions, his wife eventually admitted that Deaderick had kissed her. Deaderick said he would leave Lexington for good so "that the whole matter might be kept quiet forever."

Deaderick departed Lexington for Weaverville, a small town just outside of Asheville where his father was a college professor, within days of the confrontation, citing a "nervous condition." While there, he continued to correspond with Hege via letters, and by all accounts, the two seemed on respectful terms. If Hege's attitude toward Deaderick exuded forgiveness, that would quickly change. While Deaderick remained in Weaverville, Mrs. Hege confessed to her husband that her relationship with his friend extended far beyond one kiss; rather, it had been an affair spanning four years. Little did Deaderick know when he returned to Lexington on the evening of Saturday, March 16, that he would be dead in a matter of days.

Around noon on Tuesday, March 19, 1918, Hege left the Southern Upholstery Company to start toward his home on Hargrave Street for lunch. Hege was sitting with his wife at their kitchen table, but she eventually left to watch their oldest son leave for school. Hege continued to eat lunch for another twenty minutes or more before making his way to the sitting room. As he approached the room, he saw Deaderick sitting on the sofa and speaking to his wife. The conversation quickly turned toward the affair, with Hege telling Deaderick that he intended to alert Mrs. Deaderick of his indiscretions. He would later describe the scene in his court testimony, a summary of which appeared in the *Dispatch*:

> *After the conversation and his informing Deaderick that Mrs. Deaderick would be informed, he said Deaderick grabbed the piano seat, which was within a few feet of the end of the davenport [sofa] on which Deaderick was sitting….Hege said, at this juncture, he reached for his pistol, which was in the drawer of the library table, and that Mrs. Hege stepped from between the men. The shots then occurred….Deaderick walked toward the door. He did not see him fall, he swore, as he turned to the telephone to call up the sheriff.*

Deputy sheriff Cliff DeLapp, the son of Sheriff Alexander "Alex" DeLapp (whose other occupation was that of a singing teacher), arrived at the residence shortly after the killing to retrieve Hege. He took him to the courthouse, where the accused called for Emery Raper to serve as legal counsel. The warrant for Hege's arrest, signed by Sheriff DeLapp, alleged that "Graham Hege, with malice aforethought, did unlawfully, willfully, and feloniously kill and murder J.F. Deaderick."

As Hege waited behind bars for his preliminary hearing, Deaderick's funeral service began at 4:00 p.m. on Friday, March 22. Reverend Louis Trezevant Wilds Jr., the pastor of First Presbyterian Church, presided over the service at the Deaderick home on Fifth Avenue. Some of Lexington's most prominent citizens attended, along with Deaderick's esteemed family. By Friday night, his body had been placed on a train to begin the long haul to Marianna, Arkansas, to be buried in his wife's family plot at Cedar Heights Cemetery.

Nearly two weeks passed after Deaderick's killing before Hege appeared for a preliminary hearing. An array of prominent attorneys for both sides prepared for a dramatic battle for the ages. The upcoming hearing was the talk of the town, especially in the *Dispatch*:

> *One of the biggest legal battles in the history of Lexington—which has seen some famous ones—is in the prospect, with the life and liberty of J. Graham Hege at stake on the one hand, and the name of J. Franklin Deaderick, slain bank cashier, on the other. Hege's defense will be the "unwritten law," which south of Mason and Dixon line at least has held, to quote Emery E. Raper, "that a man who invades another's home does so at his peril." The state will contend with all its might that the dead man, who cannot speak for himself, never invaded the Hege home, at least to the extent that the public mind usually holds an "invasion" to be.*

Judge John Moyer of the Lexington Recorder's Court began the preliminary hearing at 10:00 a.m. on Saturday, March 30. With a courtroom packed to the brim, Hege, through his attorneys, pleaded not guilty. The prosecution called three witnesses to show probable cause, with the defense calling none for rebuttal.

Dr. Jarvis Terry was the first witness to take the stand, and he testified to the injuries sustained by Deaderick. He also testified that he "saw Deaderick on his way home before his death and that he was smoking a cigar." Later, at the crime scene, he said, "he found a piece of eye-glass and part of a cigar in the yard where Deaderick fell."

Lexington chief of police J.H. Mingus, who had arrived at the Hege home after the killing, testified to the victim's wounds. In describing the weapon used by Hege, he said it was a pistol "adopted by the United States Army," and it was a "powerful gun."

Last to take the stand was Emmett Witherspoon, a writer for the *Dispatch*, who interviewed Hege after the shooting. Witherspoon, who was twenty-eight years old at the time of his testimony, had arrived in Lexington in September 1915 to work for *Dispatch* publisher Henry B. Varner. He would go on to work for the publication for decades—perhaps longer than any other person—covering numerous murder trials, including that of Graham Hege. "His innate sense of honor, fairness and frequently frank but justified criticism were tempered by a keen sense of humor which enabled him to laugh—even at himself—when the occasion arose," wrote editor Fred Sink at Witherspoon's death in 1973. The reporter testified to the location of bullet holes in the walls when he visited the Hege residence. He also told the court information Hege had relayed to him during an interview at the jail.

At the conclusion of testimony, Judge Moyer ruled that "upon the trial of this case the Court finds probable cause of guilt, and Defendant is committed [to jail] without bail." Hege had to wait two months before his case was heard in superior court. His fate rested in the hands of twelve Davidson County men—ten farmers, one butcher and a painter—when his trial began in June.

As jury selection began before Superior Court judge William Jackson Adams on Monday, June 3, Hege "appeared cheerful and confident." His wife and parents were in the courtroom to offer support as the prosecution began its case against him. Also present, though supporting the state, was Mrs. Deaderick, the victim's wife.

The prosecution's case against the defendant was brief—lasting only an hour and a half—and they called only three witnesses. Among the witnesses were Dr. Jarvis Terry and Emmett Witherspoon, who both testified at the preliminary hearing, in addition to George Welborn.

Welborn, a Black barber who worked on West First Avenue near the courthouse, was a victim of violence himself in 1914. As Welborn was shaving Lexington attorney J. Ray McCrary, Della Lowe entered Welborn's barbershop and shot the barber, claiming he "caused trouble between him and his wife." Luckily, Welborn survived, but nearly four years later, he was on the stand testifying that he had sold Hege the gun that killed Deaderick. He testified that he had sold the gun to the accused man in early March, with Hege telling him "he wanted the pistol for his wife to keep in the house for protection at night when he was uptown." Prosecutors concluded their evidence at the close of Welborn's testimony.

The defense began its case with a group of powerhouse attorneys, a skilled team needed to combat the brilliance displayed by the prosecution. Their witness list was substantial, consisting of numerous character witnesses, but the most anticipated witnesses were J. Graham Hege and Edith Pugh Hege.

Hege took the stand on Monday at 4:10 p.m., when he began describing the moments before Deaderick's killing in detail. The exchange was quoted in the *Greensboro Daily News*:

Davidson County Courthouse was the location of J. Graham Hege's trial. The courthouse is depicted here between 1915 and 1930. *North Carolina Postcards, North Carolina Collection, University of North Carolina at Chapel Hill.*

He [Deaderick] *wanted to know what I wanted. I told him my wife had told me more had taken place between them than she told before, and I wanted to see him about it. I told him she told me he had had improper relations with her nearly four years and I asked him if that were true. "It isn't true," he said. "Mr. Deaderick, you know it is," my wife told him. "I'll have to admit it," he said then, "but for God's sake don't tell my wife." She must know if I have to tell her.*

When Hege was asked why he would shoot a man with whom he'd had a brotherly relationship, Hege responded simply, "To protect myself against him." The *Greensboro Daily News* reporter wrote, "Hege swore that the wrong done him through his wife had nothing whatsoever to do with his shooting, except to provide the occasion of Deaderick's excitement into assault." He claimed that, despite his friend's betrayal, he would not have killed him if he had not attempted to hit him with the piano stool.

Fiercely leading the cross-examination of Hege was forty-seven-year-old J. Ray McCrary. Fellow attorney Lister Martin described McCrary in glowing terms when he died in 1951: "His happy face and genial spirit was as familiar on the streets of Lexington as the face on the clock that hangs in the courthouse belfry; his long and distinguished service made him as much a part of Davidson County as the courthouse." Despite his "happy" disposition, the revered attorney in no way bought the idea of the plea of self-defense. Though he grilled Hege on his story and reasoning, the accused consistently remained calm on the witness stand during his almost two-hour testimony.

Mrs. Hege, who was then thirty years old, began her testimony the following morning, on Tuesday, June 4. The court excluded moments of her testimony when she alleged conversations with Deaderick, notably her first intimate encounter with him.

She recounted the first occurrence of this kind, which she says was in Nov. 1914, at her home on North Main Street, where Deaderick came, according to her story, overpowered her will, and "forced" her to submit to his will. Later she qualified the word and said "almost forced" her to submit. About once a week on an average since that date up to Feb. 4, 1918, she and the dead man had relations.

Deaderick, she testified, allegedly told her "that no men in Lexington were true to their wives, that many wives were not true to their husbands, and that men's wives in this town were doing the same things he asked her to do." She said he often arrived at her home around lunchtime or at night with a particular doorbell ring. "If her husband was at home it was a neighborly call, but if he was absent, why 'so much the better,'" wrote a *Dispatch* writer. When Deaderick spoke to her, she said, he always offered compliments, saying, "She was the only woman he had ever loved."

Under cross-examination, Mrs. Hege was asked by the prosecution why she never reported Deaderick's alleged "forceful" behavior to authorities. She responded: "I fight my own battles. I was in his power. He made me swear I would not tell my husband."

Mrs. Hege's testimony so closely resembled her husband's story that prosecutors asked "if she hadn't framed up this defense for her husband." She responded that she had done no such thing and, in fact, had not spoken to her husband since the shooting nearly three months prior.

After brief testimony from an employee of Hege, the defense rested, and the prosecution began to present their rebuttal evidence.

Grade schoolteacher (and later principal) Mrs. Banks Hankins Radcliffe, the wife of Lexington insurance man Henry Radcliffe, was the first rebuttal witness. She was the landlord of Deaderick and Hege and arrived at the home shortly after the killing. She claimed Hege said "that the shot was fired because of her [his wife's] intimacy with Deaderick." Mrs. Hege, Radcliffe said, told her, "I tried to get him [Mr. Hege] not to do it, but he is so high-tempered."

Upon the conclusion of several other witnesses' testimony on various aspects of the case which they had heard or seen, Mrs. Alma Deaderick, the victim's wife, took the stand. She testified that in early February, when Hege learned Deaderick had kissed his wife, he said to him, "If this ever gets out, I'll follow you to the ends of the earth and kill you." This statement was denied by Hege when he returned to the stand, and the taking of evidence was closed.

Closing arguments began during the afternoon of Tuesday, June 4, with solicitor John Calhoun Bower starting a marathon of speeches.

Bower, who came to Lexington in 1911, just five years prior, had prosecuted Lee Ford for killing Mel Garland; he was one of the youngest members of the prosecution but was talented, nonetheless. Speaking to the members of the jury, Bower said "that it could not, under its oath, recognize the 'unwritten law.'" That "unwritten law," described early in the trial by the defendant's counsel as "a man who invades another's home does so at his peril," was not supported by Bower. Furthermore, Bower said, "If he thought he were [*sic*] speaking to a jury which would recognize the unwritten law, he would take his seat at once. The unwritten rule means mob rule, it means anarchy."

The arguments lasted for hours on end, with attorneys from far and wide coming to speak. Perhaps the most notable were the final two: Aubrey Brooks of Greensboro for the defense and Samuel Heiskell of Knoxville, Tennessee, for the prosecution.

Brooks, once described as "the foremost and most successful lawyer in North Carolina" by North Carolina chief justice Walter Clark, had a reputation that preceded him to Lexington. His argument began during the afternoon of Thursday, June 5, with a speech the *Dispatch*'s reporter described as both "witty" and "sarcastic."

> *Combining his argument with wit and sarcasm he got the crowd into a happy frame of mind and made from this standpoint a very effective speech....Mr. Brooks declared that Deaderick intended to beat Hege into submission or beat him to death in order that his position in society and business might not be wrecked by exposure of his wrongdoing with Hege's wife.*

The attorney who would offer the closing argument for the prosecution remained uncertain for days, as Samuel Gordon Heiskell, the uncle of Deaderick, was seen by some as a possible loose cannon, according to the *Dispatch*:

> *Through the evidence and argument of counsel, he sat quietly and attentively in court and took no part in any of the examinations or cross-examinations of witnesses. He was unknown as a lawyer to any of the counsel for the state and they knew not what to expect from him. At times during the case, he had shown flashes of anger or indignation, and his associates feared that when he was unleashed he would come forth with a sensational effort.*

Ultimately, Heiskell, the most-elected mayor of Knoxville, Tennessee, and a revered attorney, offered the closing argument for the prosecution. His speech to the jury lasted longer than any other attorney's and was described by some "as one of the greatest if not the greatest legal effort ever heard in the Davidson court house [*sic*]."

> *The Tennessee lawyer began by declaring that "the friends and family of Frank Deaderick have nothing to conceal. I propose to show you that Frank Deaderick was as clean as any man who walks your streets." He covered*

Samuel G. Heiskell (1858–1923), the uncle of Deaderick, offered the closing argument for the prosecution. This portrait is housed in the City of Knoxville, Tennessee's Mayor's Office. *Tennessee Portrait Project.*

every point in this case, including a number of things overlooked or omitted by other counsel in argument, and came to the climax of his case when he vehemently declared that the case of self-defense was "a concocted affair, a pigeon stool, a cock and bull story."

Judge Adams's charge to the jury went on for more than an hour after Heiskell's closing argument. He instructed the jury that they could find Hege guilty of first-degree murder, second-degree murder or manslaughter. Alternatively, he said, they could find him not guilty of any charge. No matter the verdict, the judge warned the jury that they could not consider the so-called unwritten law, saying, "You should eliminate from your consideration of the issue any idea or notion that the prisoner had the legal right to kill because of the criminal intimacy of his wife and the deceased." The twelve members of the jury broke for lunch before beginning their deliberations.

After three and a half hours of deliberation, the courthouse bell rang to alert those who were anxiously awaiting the verdict. Sam Surratt, the foreman of the jury, announced that the jury had found John Graham Hege guilty of manslaughter. The counsel for Hege's motion to set aside and allow for a new trial due to "errors of the Court in the admission and rejection of evidence and in the Charge of the Court to the jury" was denied. Judge Adams sentenced Hege to one to four years in the state prison after pleas for mercy were made by the defense.

The following week, the *State Journal* in Raleigh published a nearly full-page opinion piece about the verdict and sentence:

> *Mr. Hege, we are told, took his indeterminate sentence of one to four years, complacently, but appealed and expressed the belief that he should have been acquitted. Our own judgment is that in conviction or acquittal, he will receive just about what is coming to him. God almighty has planted a conscious in the breast of men and so long as he lives, Graham Hege will have before him a picture which imagination*

Robert Brodnax Glenn (1854–1920), an attorney and state legislator, won the Democratic nomination for governor of North Carolina and served from 1905 to 1909. *Library of Congress.*

> *could not supply—the sightless and pathetic eyes, the widow's arms about the corpse, her lips upon the dead, the sobs of the children, the clods on the coffin, and worst of all, the portrait of himself pleading the fear of bodily harm.*

Hege's appeal to the North Carolina Supreme Court allowed his release from jail on bond. But at the fall term of the court, his appeal was dismissed.

Later, in a last-ditch effort at continued freedom, Hege petitioned Governor Thomas Walter Bickett for a pardon.

Bickett was a teacher, private attorney and attorney general before beginning his service as governor in 1917. Hege's petition that was presented to the governor bore the signatures of approximately three hundred Lexington residents. Perhaps the petition would have made a difference in the case if the victim's uncle, former North Carolina governor Robert Brodnax Glenn, not become involved. Glenn's letter to Governor Bickett, which urged him to "withstand all appeals to lessen a day of Hege's term," convinced the governor to refuse a pardon. By January 1919, Hege had begun serving his term at the state prison in Raleigh.

Mrs. Alma Deaderick, the victim's wife, moved her two sons to her hometown, Marianna, Arkansas. There, she worked as a stenographer and purchased a home. Her sons, William Franklin Deaderick and John Rodgers Deaderick, lived productive lives. Franklin worked as an engineer for the Arkansas Highway Department. Rodgers followed in his father's footsteps as a businessman and served as mayor of Forrest City, Arkansas.

Graham Hege served his year in prison, returned to Lexington and once again worked for the Southern Upholstery Company. He and Edith had another child, a son, in 1924 before they divorced. Edith settled on Hillside Drive in Lexington and supported herself as a seamstress, operating the Edith Hege Sewing Shop. Graham was remarried in June 1925 to Sallie Smith. They lived in Norfolk, Virginia, and later divorced. Graham then moved to Suffolk, Virginia, and, believing a third time might be a charm, married Lottie Bullock Peele in 1936.

In the early morning hours of Tuesday, January 28, 1941, nearly twenty-three years after he killed Frank Deaderick, Graham Hege died by suicide. His death at the age of fifty-three was caused by the inhalation of illuminating gasses, which were likely used for lighting at his home on Park Road in Suffolk. Hege's unfortunate end closed the chapter on the sad tale of two families torn apart in 1918.

10

STRUCK WITHOUT WARNING

Perhaps the saddest words that one accused of a crime could hear are "and may Almighty God have mercy on your soul." In 1924, these very words escaped the lips of Judge Thaddeus Dillard Bryson Jr. at the Davidson County Courthouse after he sentenced two men to death.

Charlie Anderson Garwood Sr. was born October 29, 1894, in Davie County. His father, John, was a farmer, and his mother, Bessie, sadly died when her son was just five years old. In 1915, Charlie married fifteen-year-old Mary Elizabeth Nail, and they settled in Shady Grove Township of Davie County. Early on, Garwood was engaged in the transportation business, offering a taxi service through Davie and the surrounding counties. He moved to Davidson County with his wife and children around 1921. Here, he expanded his business and often parked in front of the March Hotel in Lexington to wait for customers.

Cleveland Fritts and Roy Myers, residents of the western part of Davidson County, came upon the body of Garwood about a mile and a half outside of Lexington around 6:30 a.m. on Friday, August 8, 1924. As the two were driving to work, they saw a body some ten feet off the road, and thinking it was a drunk man, possibly a friend, they stopped to pick him up. As they approached, however, they saw the blood-covered, unrecognizable face of twenty-nine-year-old Garwood.

Fritts and Myers hurried to Lexington to alert Sheriff R. Bruce Talbert. At the scene, Sheriff Talbert found the body, pools of blood, fingerprints and signs of a struggle. The murder weapon, an iron bar stolen from a Lexington

Charlie Garwood's certificate of death notes he "was killed by Leak and Hale." *FamilySearch.*

blacksmith shop, was found at the scene. Almost instantaneously, law enforcement began an extensive manhunt, a search described in the *Dispatch* as going "as far north as Washington and as far south as Birmingham."

> *Sheriff Talbert and Deputy Blaylock upon arrival at the scene quickly identified the body. Information was quickly gathered that the murder had occurred about eight hours before the body was found and that Garwood's new Buick-six touring car was missing. It was evident that a cruel murder had been done. An officer rushed back to the city and the telephone and telegraph wires were made hot. North, south, east, and west, officers were asked to watch all roads for the Buick. So quickly was this search gotten under way that at 8:30 o'clock a Lancaster, S.C. man called his brother*

here over telephone to learn what had happened, saying officers there had been notified and gone out to watch all highways leading in from the north.

Amid the search, Garwood's wife and young children were alerted of the tragedy at their home near the Nokomis Cotton Mill in Lexington. Mrs. Garwood immediately suspected Jim Miller, a former passenger in her husband's taxi, as the culprit. Miller had been taken to jail after riding in Garwood's car drunk the previous Wednesday night and released the Thursday afternoon before the murder. During the investigation into the killing, Miller was held for questioning and later released after his alibi was corroborated.

County coroner Dr. Frank Lowe Mock, whose Reeds community home was not far from the crime scene, arrived to examine the body, and he and a coroner's jury began to conduct an inquest into the death. In the parlor of the Piedmont Funeral Home (then located on North Main Street, though presently located on South Main Street) Garwood's body was thoroughly examined by the jury. As was later reported in the *Dispatch*, they found the fatal injuries gruesome.

> *They found eight gaping holes in the head. There was a deep gash over the right eye. There appeared a small fracture of the skull but not one that would necessarily have caused death. A deep wound over the right ear an inch or so was next examined. Another midway between this and the right ear and a fourth where the death dealing instrument had clipped off the top of the ear. The skull bones of the entire right temple were shattered. Slightly to the left of the midline just above the base of the brain was a gaping wound, slightly oval and approximately five inches long. The cut was clean to the skull all the way and a three-inch fissure was broken in the skull, a straight regular break. Just above this wound and a little farther left was another wound, lighter than the long gash and in which there was no breaking of bone.*

Within hours of the discovery of the body, Greensboro policemen Harris and Oakley had recovered the victim's blood-covered Buick near the passenger station in that city. After the car was found, two Greensboro men, Will McClode and Ernest Dinkins, were taken into police custody for questioning. The discovery of a pair of stained—though freshly washed—overalls behind McClode's home made police suspicious, but he was ultimately released shortly after his arrest. Dinkins, on the other hand, had in his possession "a piece of paper bearing the license plate number of the car of the dead man." He claimed he had received the paper from an acquaintance, leading law enforcement to the names of two suspects: John Leak (note that despite newspaper accounts spelling his surname "Leake," numerous court documents and legal records drop the "e" from his name) and Kenneth Hale. Leak and Hale were both young Black men, though they were hardly old enough to be referred to as men, despite the severity of the crime of which they were accused.

By the early morning of Saturday, August 9, Hale was placed under arrest near railroad tracks in Charlotte. Hale and Leak ran as Charlotte police officers approached them, "but Hale lost his nerve at the sight of Detective Cate's revolver and waited for officers to arrest him." Leak managed to escape the officers' gunshots and bloodhounds by running through swamplands. Meanwhile, Hale, a native of Charleston, West Virginia, freely spoke to police, laying blame at the feet of Leak, according to the *Greensboro Daily News*:

> *Hale, who looks to be about 20 years of age, talked freely of the killing, admitting that he and Leak employed Garwood to carry them out a short distance from Lexington on Thursday night. Garwood resisted an effort to rob him, Hale said, and Leak beat him to death with a heavy iron bar. Hale denied, repeatedly, that he had anything to do with the killing, placing all the blame on Leak.*

On the eve of Garwood's funeral, Governor Cameron Morrison offered a $400 reward for the capture of Leak, with the City of Lexington and Davidson County later contributing an additional $400. The funeral began at 3:00 p.m. on Sunday, August 10, in the Advance community of Davie County. As the crowds gathered to grieve, Leak remained on the lam, and Hale sat behind bars in the Charlotte jail.

Thirty-five-year-old Issac Littleton Blaylock, the chief deputy sheriff of Davidson County, took the helm of the search for John Leak. After receiving a tip, Blaylock decided to make a trip to Leak's former home in Laurens County, South Carolina. The trip led him to the arrest of Leak on August 15, exactly one week after Fritts and Myers discovered Garwood's body. The *Dispatch* described, in detail, the capture at the home of Carroll Drayton Nance Sr.

> *Leake had gone back to the refuge of the white man who had practically reared him, and for whom he had worked in his boyhood days. "Boss,*

I've come back to stay with you this time," Mr. Nance told officers Leake remarked to him as he greeted him on Sunday morning, August 10. The negro had arrived on the farm sometime Saturday night. Mr. Nance, who is a large planter and is now a candidate for the state senate in his district, had not learned of Leake's crime until after the officers had arrived and placed the negro under arrest. He could hardly restrain his indignation when he learned what had taken place. "Boss, I'll be out of this and come back soon," Leake said to Mr. Nance as they were ready to depart. "I hope I may never see you again," replied the planter.

With Chief Deputy Blaylock's nephew Lee Hancock driving the car to Charlotte from South Carolina, the prisoner sat in the passenger seat and begged not to be taken to Lexington. He cried, "I'm not ready to die!" Blaylock sat in the back seat with a pistol, anticipating any sudden moves from Leak. The men made it safely to Charlotte, and the prisoner then went into the custody of Sheriff Talbert around 2:55 p.m. Leak, after seeing his codefendant, said, "I've been hearing Mr. Charlie hollar [*sic*]," referring to their victim.

Guarded by Talbert and Blaylock and handcuffed together, the prisoners, Hale and Leak, made the trip to Greensboro from Charlotte. Once they arrived in Greensboro, the men were placed in separate cells, free to blame the other for Garwood's death. According to the *Greensboro Daily News*, Leak, specifically, used his time in custody to be a chatterbox to the press and anyone who would listen.

Each knows that the other is trying to fasten the murder on him. Both realize the seriousness of their positions. Leake talks volubly and in the greatest detail. He pours out his story, words tumbling after each other. He recites details, remembers exact figures, dates, hours, days, numbers, and every movement taken by himself or by Hale. Hale won't talk so much. He is almost surly. Asked a definite question he will answer but he does not volunteer much. Leak volunteers everything.

After the grand jury returned a true bill of indictment for murder against Leak and Hale, Sheriff Talbert retrieved the prisoners from the Guilford County Jail and brought them to Lexington. And it was on Monday, August 18, when Judge Bryson, whose father is the namesake of Bryson City, took the bench for the defendants' arraignment.

Leak and Hale's arraignment began after the lunch recess in the crowded upstairs courtroom. All eyes were on the accused men as they walked through the doors. "They entered the courtroom with steady tread and not the slightest show of fear or nervousness. In fact, they gave the appearance of not knowing what it was all about," according to the *Greensboro Daily News*. When Judge Bryson asked the men their plea, they both pleaded guilty to being in the car of Garwood but not guilty of Garwood's murder. The judge accepted both pleas of not guilty and set the hearing for the following Wednesday. The sheriff quickly bundled Leak and Hale into a car headed straight for the Guilford County Jail to prevent violence in a town full of emotion, though it was apparently law-abiding.

> *While the people of Davidson County have been greatly aroused over the murder of young Garwood, a popular fellow with a wife and several small children, there have been no open threats of violence so far as could be learned today, and no trouble is anticipated. The people of Davidson County are a law-abiding people and the certainty of a speedy and fair trial for the accused negroes has doubtless had much to do with keeping down any reckless talk of violence. The feeling here is that the law should take its course—and the law will take its course.*

Just before 10:00 a.m. on Wednesday, August 20, 1924, John Leak and Kenneth Hale were escorted into the courtroom to face a trial for their lives. One newspaper reporter described the crowd as being so great that the spectators were "packed in like sardines." C.M. Brown, a member of the large crowd and the editor of the *Greensboro Daily Record*, wrote, "They were standing six or seven feet deep all around the bar, were crowded in back of the jury boxes, aisles were packed and windows contained all they would hold. Many even refused to leave for lunch and stayed put so as to have seats."

As jury selection began, the defense teams (Leak and Hale retaining separate counsel) quickly realized their challenge ahead. When questioning potential jurors, the attorneys found "almost a solid wall of expressed belief that their clients are guilty of the serious charge against them." Ultimately, ten farmers, a merchant and a furniture worker were selected as jurors by 3:20 p.m. Reports in the *Greensboro Daily News* explained that each juror stated opinions of the defendants' guilt.

> *Every man who sits on that jury swore under oath today that he had either read or heard of the killing and that he had formed the opinion that both negroes are guilty. Those who compose the jury, however, stated under oath*

John Leak and Kenneth Hale willingly posed for a photograph in the prisoners' room of the Davidson County Courthouse while on trial for murder. *From the* Dispatch, *August 25, 1924.*

that they could sit on the jury, hear the evidence, argument of counsel, and charge of the court, and render a fair and impartial verdict.

Solicitor James Franklin Spruill, then forty-one years old, quickly paved the way for his case before the jury. The crux of his argument stood on the premise that "Leak and Hale plotted the death of the young taxi driver with robbery as the motive; that they lured him to a lonely spot two or three miles from Lexington and there beat him to death with an iron bar. It purposes to show that the iron bar was procured by Hale for that purpose; that both Hale and Leak were not working; that they had no money and that they intended to kill Garwood when hired him to take them to Dennis Smith's home on the night of August 7." A "good-natured" Judge Bryson warned the crowd to behave properly before the prosecutor began his case by calling Mrs. Mary Elizabeth Garwood, the victim's wife.

Mrs. Garwood, dressed in mourning clothes of all black, testified that her husband had often carried a substantial amount of money. She stated that the Wednesday night before the murder, they counted his money together, her husband having $152 in his pockets. Mrs. Garwood said she last saw him alive around 10:00 a.m. Thursday, August 7, as he brought her two bushels of peaches to their home. Within twenty-four hours, she learned that her husband was dead.

The prosecution next called Pearl Falls, the owner of a boardinghouse near the railroad depot, who testified that Leak and Hale had stayed at her home the week of the killing. Wiley Lewis followed Falls's testimony, saying he had heard Hale say the night before Garwood's murder, "I'm broke now, but before Saturday night I'll have some money if I have to kill some s— of a b—." Three additional witnesses were called on the first day of trial, and they testified that they saw Leak and Hale together in the days leading up to the killing.

More than twenty witnesses for the prosecution testified on the second day of trial, August 21, 1924, a day described as being "tremendously hot." It was so hot, in fact, that by midafternoon, after some rain had fallen in Lexington, "the humid air, rising from the heated sidewalks on which the rain fell, filled the courtroom and for about half an hour the atmosphere was almost unendurable." The temperature was not the only thing running high in the courtroom, as emotions rose each day of the trial. Within an hour of the beginning of court, Leak's mother had to leave the courthouse due to her loud crying and praying during testimony. The trial went on, with prosecutors piecing together their case witness by witness.

Blacksmiths Wade McCrary and Robert Leonard took the stand and broached the subject of the murder weapon. They both testified that they had witnessed Leak take an iron bar, the eventual murder weapon, from their shop in Lexington.

Jule Henderson, an older gentleman who lived on Cotton Grove Road in Lexington, rode in the car with Garwood and the two alleged killers the night of the murder. However, he was not able to identify Hale and Leak as his two copassengers.

Perhaps one of the most informative witnesses of the day was Aiken Bruce of Greensboro. The *Greensboro Daily News* recounted his testimony:

Aiken Bruce, Greensboro negro, told of John Leak coming to his home on East Washington Street about midnight Thursday night of the murder for a suit of clothes he had left in Bruce's house, where Leak had spent Sunday and Monday prior to the murder. "Leak came in and asked for his clothes," said Bruce. "He also asked for a cigarette and a match, which I gave him. When I was a little slow in handing him a cigarette he said he was in a hurry. He said, "I've killed a man." I said, "No you haven't, you're only foolin'," but he said, "I hope God may strike me dead if I ain't."

The final witness of the day, Chief Deputy Sheriff Isaac Littleton Blaylock, told the court the stories the defendants had allegedly relayed to him after they were arrested. A reporter for the *Winston-Salem Journal* quoted his in-detail testimony, which lasted until around 5:00 p.m.

Leake said he was in front, Hale behind. Out on the Mocksville road Hale struck Garwood twice and Leake brought the car to a stop, as Hale continued to pound on the bleeding victim. "Don't kill him," Leake told the deputy he implored, it was recounted. "Shut your damn mouth," was Hale's reply. Hale dragged the body from the car according to this version. Leake drove the car away and a short distance from the spot Hale said, "What the hell's the use to kill a man and not get his money?" Leake said the car was turned and driven back, and that Garwood was up and groaning. Hale leaped out and there was a sound of blows. "I got him," said Hale as he returned to the car. A quarter of a mile away, according to this reproduction of Leake's story, Hale remarked, "Stop, I left that damn piece of iron in the road," Leake said, testified the witness, that he drove back, threw the lights of the car on the iron, passed the car over it, and Hale got out and threw it into the stubble. Hale told the deputy, it was testified, that Leake struck Garwood first with a .45 revolver and then a piece of iron. Hale said he and Garwood made outcry and Leake told him to "shut up or I'll kill you."

When Blaylock's testimony concluded, Judge Bryson adjourned court and instructed Sheriff Talbert to return the prisoners to the Guilford County Jail. Soon, though, fear crept into the minds of the defendants when the car that was to take them back to their temporary home arrived late. "They strained the chain by which Sheriff Talbert held them much as do hunting dogs," wrote the *Greensboro Daily News* reporter. "They begged him to keep them from the crowd. Frank terror was displayed on their faces." Despite the great

Chief Deputy Sheriff Isaac Littleton Blaylock (1889– 1957) served as one of the prosecution's primary witnesses during the trial. *From the* Dispatch, *August 25, 1924.*

fear experienced by the defendants that harm may come their way, particularly lynching, Leak and Hale safely made it to Greensboro and returned to Lexington the following morning.

The final day of testimony saw Deputy Blaylock and Sheriff Talbert, among others, called to take the stand before the state rested its case on the afternoon of Friday, August 22, 1924. The defendants called no witnesses to testify, and Orville Hackney, the counsel for Kenneth Hale, began closing arguments.

Twenty-nine-year-old Hackney was licensed to practice law in 1915 and worked as an attorney in Charleston, West Virginia. In his argument, which was no more than thirty minutes long, he attempted to use Hale's youth as a defense, saying that Leak likely led the killing. "No man could perhaps tell which killed Charlie Garwood or whether both killed," said Hackney, concluding that if reasonable doubt existed, his client should be found not guilty.

As Mrs. Garwood sat and wept, Archibel "Archie" Elledge of Winston-Salem argued that the defendants should be found guilty and sentenced to death. "No more heinous crime was ever committed in North Carolina than this," argued Elledge. "Society demands these murderers should pay with their lives."

Marshall Mott, who, just a few years later, left the law to become a minister, gave the last and longest argument of the day for John Leak. Mott pinned "the worst crime that has been committed in North Carolina" on Hale, who he described as a "foul, festered liar and murderer," according to the *Twin City Sentinel.*

> *John Leake is guilty of larceny of a car, guilty of accessory after murder, of robbery of money—guilty of conduct unbecoming to any human being, but when he tells the truth unvarnished like God made it, give him the benefit....If John Leake killed Charlie Garwood he was crazy.*

For Hale, the argument he fretted over the most was that of Solicitor J. Frank Spruill. As Sheriff Talbert transported the defendants back to

Greensboro after court, Hale remarked, "The thing I dread is that little prosecutor. I know what he's goin' to say. He's goin' to say, 'Hide 'em.' And he ain't goin' to mean hide 'em in Davidson County, either. He's goin' to mean hide 'em six feet under the ground." Indeed, Spruill did make such an argument, according to the *Dispatch*.

> *"The County of Davidson and the state of North Carolina want no compromise verdict, but a verdict of first degree murder against both and wants it promptly," asserted the solicitor to the jury near the end of his argument. "They could have taken his car, money and spared his life, but they were too hellish," he exclaimed. "They would have destroyed any other man in the county as quickly. They are destroyers of society." Men and women wept as Mr. Spruill described the crime and its results. The defendants sat apparently little concerned during the dramatic recital.*

After Mott spoke a second time for Leak, David Salisbury of Charleston, West Virginia, cocounsel for Hale, gave the final closing argument of the trial. Appearing in court at the request of his client's mother and grandmother, Salisbury described Hale as "a half-witted ignorant black boy." He asked the jury to "find John Leake guilty of murder and send him to the electric chair." He pleaded for Hale to be found guilty of second-degree murder and saved from the death penalty.

The deliberation of the jury began at 3:15 p.m. on Saturday, August 23, 1924, after a nearly two-hour charge offered by Judge Bryson. By 3:42 p.m.—just twenty-seven minutes later—the twelve jurors had determined the fate of the accused. "We the jury find John Leake guilty of murder in the first degree," came the words of John J. McCuiston, the foreman of the jury. The clerk of superior court Edward C. Byerly (who, while having just been elected in 1922, would go on to serve as clerk for twenty-four years) asked the foreman, "What say you as to Kenneth Hale?" Hale, the foreman said, was also guilty of first-degree murder. When the clerk polled the jury, the verdict was unanimous, and the defendants' motion to set aside the verdict was denied.

In a 1972 news article, the *Dispatch* told of what happened next. As the jury deliberated, Emmett E. Witherspoon, the reporter who was covering the trial for the publication, prepared two alternative headlines based on the verdict. He had gone so far as to approach Judge Bryson in his chambers while the jury was out to ask what the execution date would be for the defendants if they were found guilty. When the jury announced the guilty verdict, a piece of paper that bore the not-yet-announced execution date was thrown from the courtroom window. "Allen (Toby) Myers of the composing room was stationed on the back steps of the courthouse, leaped into the air, grabbed the note and hit the ground running. Within hardly more than five minutes copies of the extra had reached the courtroom," reads the *Dispatch* article. As the prisoners waited for sentencing in the prisoners' room, Mayor Charles Young read them their execution date from the newspaper. "How did that paper know this, when the judge hasn't told us?" asked Leak or Hale. Moments later, just after 4:30 p.m., Judge Bryson sentenced both men to death by electrocution in Raleigh between 4:00 a.m. and 4:00 p.m. on October 9, 1924. Ernest Dinkins of Greensboro, who had attempted to lead officers away from Leak and Hale, pleaded guilty to being an accessory after a murder and an accessory after a highway robbery. He was sentenced to ten years in the state prison.

Within minutes, Sheriff Talbert was in a car headed for the state prison with his prisoners. However, it was not an uneventful ride to Raleigh. The sheriff had not even made it out of the county when the car was involved in a traffic accident in Thomasville. The damages sustained left the car unable to make the trip to the prison, and businessman Fred Cox of Lexington picked up the sheriff and his prisoners. Unknown to Cox, he would allegedly become a witness to a confession.

As the story goes, Cox drove, which allowed Sheriff Talbert to talk to Leak and Hale. The sheriff asked them, "Haven't I treated you well and protected both of your lives?" Both men responded, "Yes." "Then tell me the truth before I turn you over at the state prison," said the sheriff. They both replied with their previously stated stories. "You know neither of you are telling the truth, for both of you were not on the front seat at the time," remarked Talbert, which led Hale to talk. The confession was quoted in the *Dispatch*:

We both planned the killing. I was on the back seat and struck the first lick. Mr. Garwood hollered and John Leake grabbed him by the throat. I struck him with the iron, and John said, "Let me have that iron. You don't know how to kill him, I've done this before." John hit him several times with the iron, and we both dragged him out of the car. When we drove back by we heard him groan and John got out and took a rock and broke in his head. I could hear the skull crash.

The sheriff reported that after Hale had said his peace, he turned to Leak and asked, "Is this how it happened, John?" John responded, "Yes, that's the

THE STATE'S PRISON
Raleigh, North Carolina

To *E. C. Byrly* , Clerk of the Superior Court

of *Davidson* County:

We do hereby certify that *Kenneth Hale & John Leak* was

duly electrocuted on *Monday* the *5* day of *January* 19 *25*

in accordance with law and in execution of the judgment pronounced against him at the

August 192 *4* term of the Superior Court of *Davidson* County,

which judgment, on appeal, was affirmed by the Supreme Court, and which date was

fixed for the electrocution by the Governor in accordance with law.

Witness our hands this the *5th* day of *January* 19 *25*

S. J. Busbee
Warden of State's Prison

J. N. Norman n. d.
Physician of State's Prison

The following persons were present and acted as witnesses:

Eo. F. Smith   *R. B. Talbert*

Raymond Bowen   *Mrs. R. B. Talbert*

J. C. Bodenhamer   *W. H. Brown*

Charlie Sells   *M. F. Talbert*

Mr. G. Hartley   *R. L. Gray jr*

John F. Foard   *Blackburn W. Johnson*

This letter to clerk of superior court Edward C. Byerly, dated January 5, 1925, informs the clerk that Leak and Hale were executed. *State Archives of North Carolina.*

truth. I'd thought before I'd tell it but it was so brutal I just didn't want to talk about it." The men told the sheriff about how they'd planned the murder, first selecting a different Lexington taxi driver, but Leak suggested Garwood because he knew "he carries a roll [of cash] all the time." But while they were planning, Hale said he wished not to kill him. Leak said, "No, let's kill him. Dead men tell no stories." Sheriff Talbert said that not only did Leak confess to Garwood's murder, but he also confessed he intended to return to Lexington after the murder to kill five more people and end his criminal career in a "blaze of glory." In just seventeen days, Sheriff Talbert, the namesake of Talbert Boulevard in Lexington, had arrested two murderers, seen them both convicted and allegedly received a full confession by the time he arrived in Raleigh.

When the time arrived for Leak and Hale to face death, prison warden Sam Busbee was in California, seeking the capture of escaped convict James Walter Peacock. Peacock, a physician formerly of Davidson County, had killed Thomasville chief of police John Taylor in cold blood in 1921. The search for Peacock led Governor Cameron Morrison to delay the executions of Leak and Hale until November 10. In November, Hale sought a commutation of his death sentence to life in prison, so Governor Morrison again delayed the execution to review the case. Despite Hale's plea for mercy, January 5, 1925, became the date that John Leak and Kenneth Hale would face the electric chair.

At 10:25 a.m. on Monday, January 5, 1925, Kenneth Hale walked into the room where he would meet his end, singing spirituals and telling those around him goodbye. "Good Lord, take me when I come to thee," said Hale before he was shocked four times with 1,800 volts of electricity. The victim's brother Joe Garwood was present and fainted; he eventually left the room as the electrical currents went through Hale's body. Some ten minutes later, when Garwood knocked on the door to witness Leak's death at 10:37 a.m., he was denied admission. In just over ten minutes, two young men's lives were over as payment for the crime of which they were convicted.

Mary Garwood gave birth to a baby boy on February 17, 1925, a month after her husband's killers faced their deaths. She named him Charlie Anderson Garwood Jr., after his father. Tragically, two months later, the young Garwood died. Mrs. Garwood remarried in 1927 and lived a long life before eventually dying in 1985. Despite more than six decades passing since her first husband's death, she was buried with him in the Advance community of Davie County. Above her gravestone inscription is that of Charlie Anderson Garwood Sr.: "MURDERED AUG. 7, 1924."

11
HUNTING LEADS TO FEUDING

Hundreds of miles from Davidson County, along the West Virginia and Kentucky border, are the remnants of one of the bloodiest family feuds in history. Yes, it is the sad story of the Hatfields and McCoys of which I write. But in Thomasville, many years ago, another feud between two families ended in bloodshed on Fisher Ferry Street.

The feuding between the Hedrick and Kindley families began to brew in 1925, first between Lartha "Larthy" Lee Hedrick and Sam Kindley. While Hedrick was hunting on land cared for by the Kindleys in the fall of 1925, Kindley fired a gun in his direction to scare him away. Acting in revenge, Hedrick and an accomplice returned to the farm later in the day and gave Sam Kindley a "terrible beating." Neither Hedrick nor his counterpart faced prosecution for the assault, and by all accounts, it seemed both families intended to let bygones be bygones—that is until March 1926.

Hedrick, an ice wagon driver for Joseph William Boyles, the owner of the Thomasville Bottling Company, was working when he met Kindley in front of Everhart's Store on Thursday, March 25, 1926. Around 1:00 p.m., following an intense exchange of words, Hedrick stabbed John Kindley, the father of his enemy Sam Kindley, in the heart on Fisher Ferry Street. Fifty-six-year-old Kindley was lying dead in a pool of blood when Drs. J. Edward Hobgood and Raymond Yokeley arrived.

Within moments, Hedrick fled the scene, going through some woods toward his home on Randolph Street. Hedrick's wife denied her husband was home when Thomasville police officers and Sheriff R. Bruce Talbert arrived, but upon entry, they found him refusing to climb down from the

B.V.S.—Form 7

NORTH CAROLINA STATE BOARD OF HEALTH
BUREAU OF VITAL STATISTICS

STANDARD CERTIFICATE OF DEATH

172

Registration District No. 29-2201

1 PLACE OF DEATH
County Davidson
Township Thomasville
City Thomasville

Register No. 20

2 FULL NAME John G. Kindley

(a) Residence. No.
(Usual place of abode)

PERSONAL AND STATISTICAL PARTICULARS

3 Sex Male
4 Color or Race White
5 Single, Married, Widowed, or Divorced (write the word) Widowed

5a If married, widowed, or divorced
Husband of
(or) Wife of

6 Date of birth (month, day, and year) June 8 1869

7 Age 50 years, Months 9, Days 7

8 Occupation of deceased
(a) Trade, Profession, or particular kind of work Farmer

9 Birthplace (city or town) Randolph Co.

10 Name of Father Illigitimate.

11 Birthplace of Father (city or town)

12 Maiden Name of Mother Delila Kindley

13 Birthplace of Mother (city or town) Randolph Co.

14 Informant Sam Kindley
(Address) Thomasville Rt. 4 N.C.

15 Filed 3/31 1926 B.H.Harris

MEDICAL CERTIFICATE OF DEATH

16 Date of Death (month, day, and year) March 25 1926

17 I HEREBY CERTIFY, That I attended deceased from March 23 1926 to Mar 25 1926 that I last saw him alive March 25 1926 and that death occurred, on the date stated above, at 1 P. m.

The CAUSE OF DEATH was as follows:
Dead when seen murdered — was stabbed in chest

Contributory (SECONDARY)

(Signed) J.V. Yokeley M.D.
3/25, 1926 (Address) Thomasville N.C.

19 Place of Burial, Cremation, or removal Plesant Grove
Date of Burial 3=28 1926

20 Undertaker W W Russell
Address Thomasville

REGISTRAR

John Kindley's certificate of death was modified at some point to read he "was stabbed in heart with knife by someone now serving time in State Prison." *FamilySearch*.

home's loft. After much concern and a gathering of numerous people around the home, Hedrick surrendered to law enforcement. Tearfully, he changed his clothing before he was escorted to jail.

Dr. Frank Mock, the county coroner, summoned a coroner's jury the next day. D.S. Long, a sign painter, and Virgie Upton, a child, served as witnesses in the hearing to determine if Hedrick should go before the grand jury for possible indictment. They "testified that Hedrick, using vile language, advanced upon Kindley, drawing his pocket knife and stabbing his victim in the left side," wrote a *Winston-Salem Journal* reporter. Drs. Mock and Yokeley stated that after examination, they determined "that the blade of the knife had penetrated to a depth of five inches, entering the cavity of the heart, and that the gash was five inches in length at the surface." Ultimately, the coroner's jury determined the case should proceed to the grand jury.

Left: Robert Bruce Talbert (1889–1979) was the sheriff of Davidson County from 1922 to 1926. Later, he served as the chief of police in Lexington. *From the* Dispatch, *September 7, 1922.*

Right: Clyde Hoey (1877–1954) began his career as a newspaperman but became an attorney and respected politician. *Library of Congress, Prints & Photographs Division, photograph by Harris & Ewing (reproduction number, e.g., LC-USZ62-123456).*

As the thirty-year-old Hedrick awaited trial, early predictions suggested his would be a case to remember. A correspondent for the *Winston-Salem Journal* wrote in mid-April that Hedrick would "offer a stout defense at his trial."

> *He will plead self-defense on the contention that the older man* [Kindley] *called him a vile name and attacked him with a knife without cause. A suit of overalls worn by Hedrick at the time will probably be an important exhibit in* [sic] *his behalf. Hedrick stated after his arrest, according to the sheriff, that Kindley made the gashes in the overalls with a knife. The State will charge that Hedrick was the aggressor all the way, and that it was he that applied the epithet to Kindley and began the cutting, it is understood. The State will also deny that Kindley cut Hedrick's overalls, according to present plans.*

Judge Thomas Brown Finley of Wilkes County arrived in Lexington on Monday, May 3, and set out to hear the matter of the *State v. Hedrick* on Wednesday. The prosecutors for the state were solicitor J. Franklin Spruill and

John Raymond McCrary, both of Lexington, and Clyde Hoey of Shelby (the future governor of North Carolina from 1937 to 1941 who later died in his Senate office in Washington, D.C., in 1954). Representing the defendant were the revered Lexington firms Raper and Raper, and Phillips and Bower.

Testifying for the state were numerous witnesses, including D.S. Long and Virgie Upton, who had previously testified before the coroner's jury. Ross Gallimore, also an eyewitness, testified to much the same story as Long and Upton. The *Greensboro Daily News* summarized their stories:

> *As Kindley walked by where Hedrick and two others were sitting on the steps of a Thomasville store, the former gave a friendly greeting that Hedrick returned with an epithet and oath. Long and Gallimore testified Kindley turned around and asked if the oath was intended for him and that Hedrick told him he had better move on. Kindley continued to face Hedrick, and the latter advanced on him…opening his knife as he came. Kindley also took a knife from his pocket, said both witnesses, but put it back at the command of Hedrick. Hedrick then slapped Kindley, said both witnesses, and Kindley leaned over as if to grab for a piece of plank. Hedrick forbade the older man to pick up anything and as Kindley raised back up without the plank, Hedrick cut him in the left side, both witnesses said.*

After hearing testimonies from several supporting witnesses for the prosecution, the defense began their case with many character witnesses and testimony from the defendant himself.

> *Hedrick, testifying today, said that Kindley called him and applied a vile epithet, that he went toward Kindley and the latter approached him, with opened knife in his hand. A few words passed and Kindley began cutting at him, whereupon he struck the older man once with his knife, producing death. Hedrick on cross-examination denied that he made a small wound in his hand and tore his overalls on a barbed wire fence he crossed on his way home after the killing. He claimed that cuts in the overalls, exhibited in court, were made by Kindley. His shirt and undershirt also were cut, he testified, but the skin was not marked.*

Upon the conclusion of testimonies and closing arguments, the jury began their deliberations around 6:00 p.m. on Friday, May 7, 1926. After being deadlocked between charges of first- and second-degree murder, the jury found the defendant guilty of second-degree murder on Saturday morning.

The counsel for the defendant pleaded for mercy from Judge Finley in sentencing. Emotionally, Emery Raper asked for leniency, and then John Bower began his argument, "saying that [Hedrick's] life, on the whole, had been good and that he was [a] deserving object for the mercy of the judge." Alternatively, the prosecution asked for a hefty sentence, with the intention of making an example of Hedrick in the Thomasville community. His honor then handed down a maximum thirty-year sentence to Larthy Hedrick.

> *As the group began to break up, there remained by the side of the convicted young man his aging father, whose quiet loyalty had been his throughout the fight to escape even a more dire fate than that accorded. There might have been a stray tear…escaping from the half-shut eyes of the slightly bowed man, who was perhaps thinking of the task ahead of him of going back to Thomasville to tell his bedridden wife and the mother of an unfortunate son of the punishment that had been meted out at the hands of the state that had been offended.*

In passing down his sentence, Judge Finley earned respect—at the very least—from the press. An editorial in the *Greensboro Record* praised him for his decision: "Judge Finley and the court are to be commended for the heavy punishment meted out to the slayer in this case. We recall the details of this

Lartha "Larthy" Lee Hedrick left Davidson County for the state prison in Raleigh after his guilty verdict. *North Carolina Postcards, North Carolina Collection, University of North Carolina at Chapel Hill.*

useless and indefensible slaying well. Hedrick might easily have defended himself against the assault he claimed to have feared and was unjustified in his deadly assault on Kindley. Unless the penalties provided by our laws are applied, human life will become even cheaper than it is now." The defendant himself showed no issue with the verdict or the sentence and refrained from appealing his case.

Hedrick began serving his sentence at the North Carolina State Penitentiary in Raleigh shortly after his trial. Here, officials described him as a "model prisoner" who was "held in high esteem." In fact, when his father, Alex Hedrick, died in July 1929, he was allowed to go home for the funeral without the supervision of guards.

Upon his release from prison, Hedrick returned to Thomasville and again worked at the Thomasville Bottling Company but moved to neighboring Montgomery County around 1934. In a strange turn of events, Lartha Lee Hedrick died on March 4, 1935, in Thomasville at just thirty-nine years old. His cause of death was an infection caused by injuries sustained to his arm and a dislocated elbow.

Immediately following Herick's death, rumors swirled around the county that he "had made a statement concerning the recent Biscoe bank robbery" and that such was the cause of his injuries. The robbery, which netted the robbers some $1,200 (equivalent to approximately $27,000 today), occurred in February 1935. The getaway car was found abandoned near Denton with no trace of its occupants.

Despite rumors, the sheriff's office disputed claims that Hedrick was involved, believing his injuries were the results of an altercation in Montgomery County. Allegedly, though, Hedrick claimed before his death to "have fallen over a stump in the darkness." No matter the cause, Hedrick's mysterious death gave an unexpected close to a feud between two families long ago.

12

MURDER, MANSLAUGHTER OR ASSAULT

Between 1914 and 1918, a deadly war raged. World War I claimed millions of soldiers' lives before concluding on November 11, 1918, a day now set aside as Veterans' Day. A young, brown-eyed barber from Davidson County, Private Ernest Irvin Michael, served in this conflict. He survived the war, married and fathered eight children before meeting an untimely, scandalous death in 1936.

Following a Sunday afternoon drive on January 12, 1936, forty-six-year-old Michael drowned in High Rock Lake during a fight with his copassenger, Harrison C. Rogers. Efforts to resuscitate Michael were unsuccessful after the elderly Robert John "Uncle Bob" Lookabill, an esteemed resident of the Southmont community, recovered Michael's body from about twelve feet of water.

Dr. Jarvis R. Terry, the county coroner, summoned a coroner's jury to convene at the Piedmont Funeral Home in Lexington on Monday. Rogers voluntarily made a statement to the jury about his version of events.

> *He said that he and Mrs. Rogers had driven to Lexington yesterday morning* [Sunday], *reaching here about eleven o'clock. Mrs. Rogers was driving, he said. He said that they picked up Michael and Seabo Wilson here and then drove by the Junior Home and down through Silver Hill Township and back to the lower bridge over the Abbotts Creek channel, he said, and Michael got out and said he wouldn't ride any farther. Rogers said he got out to try and get Michael back into the car, that Michael struck him on*

Ernest Michael's certificate of death lists his cause of death as "drowning." Dr. Jarvis Terry notes the death was accidental. *FamilySearch.*

the head with a bottle and then got his knife. They clinched, he said, fell over the guard fence, and rolled down the rock-covered fill about fifteen feet and into the water. Rogers said he tried to get Michael out of the water and struggled with him until they were about twenty feet from shore when he was forced to give up the rescue effort and swim out.

After hearing evidence, the jury returned a verdict that "death came from drowning resulting from a fight with Rogers." At nearly fifty years old, Rogers, a former member of the Lexington police force and a railway officer in Spencer, was arrested for murder.

Rogers's time in Lexington as a police officer seems to have been a time of relative calm, except for a close encounter with death in 1926. Nearly ten years before he himself faced a murder charge, Rogers was on the other end of John Carter's knife when he attempted to arrest the latter. The *Dispatch* reported that "Rogers' coat was slashed [to] almost shreds in front and he received a number of light knife wounds, and two that required stitches to close." As luck would have it, a dull knife and Rogers's proximity to his assailant were credited with saving him. But in 1936, neither Rogers nor his victim, Ernest Michael, would be so lucky.

Dwight Luther Pickard, the judge of the county court since 1934, presided over Rogers's preliminary hearing the following Friday morning before a packed courtroom. The prosecutors were solicitor J. Lee Wilson and John Bower, while the defendant's counselors were Frank Spruill and Hubert E. Olive Sr. In Olive, a man still early in his career, Rogers would find an invaluable ally. Standing six feet tall with a "powerful, resonant voice," Olive was described as having a "spectacular personality in the courtroom." His wife, Anne Olive, was once quoted as saying,

Hubert Ethridge Olive Sr. (1895–1972) was an attorney, state legislator and judge before he narrowly lost the Democratic nomination for governor in 1952. *From the* Annual of the Baptist State Convention of North Carolina.

"There are two things Hubert can't do—tip-toe nor whisper." Years later, Olive would take office as a superior court judge and, later, as a district court judge. His son Hubert E. Olive Jr. followed his father's footsteps and became a district court judge, serving for over a decade before passing away in 2023 at the age of ninety-four.

The state opened its case with the testimony of Herbert McCulloch and Grady Wilson, who both testified they witnessed Rogers drinking whiskey in Lexington before the ill-fated car ride. Seabo Wilson, a copassenger of Rogers and Michael, was the next witness to take the stand. His testimony was recalled in the *Dispatch*.

> *Seabo Wilson testified that Mr. Michael came for him at the Lanning home near Holt School and that he got in the car and they started for the Junior Home bridge....There it was suggested by Michael, he said, that they see the backwaters of the lake. They took the Silver Hill road and stopped at the home of Mrs. Angeline Cross where Michael attempted to purchase produce. From there, they went on, coming into the main highway below Southmont, and headed back toward Lexington. Rogers and Michael were joking and were teasing each other, he said....Just as they approached the*

bridge, Wilson said Rogers said, "You've gone far enough," and reaching to the dashboard of the car, took the key from the lock. As the car slowed almost to a stop, Wilson opened the door and started across the bridge, as he thought there was going to be trouble and did not wish to become involved.

Four young women, teachers at the Denton School, were approaching the bridge in their car when they saw another blocking the roadway and two men and a woman walking across the bridge. And though the teachers passed the vehicle, Miss Lucille Lohr testified that "when she next saw the two men [Michael and Rogers], they were locked together in a scuffle and fell over the wire guard at the northern end of the bridge." As they drove by, Mrs. Rogers asked for help, and the women headed to Southmont for assistance.

The young schoolteachers from Denton sought help from Amos Rich, a teacher at the Southmont School, along with two other men from Southmont. As they arrived on the scene, the gentlemen met Rogers and his wife on the bridge. Rich testified that Rogers "was bleeding profusely from a cut over an eye and that his shirt and face were very bloody," as he told them of the location of Michael's body in the lake.

Deputy Sheriff Albert Alexander Graves (known affectionately as "Peg") of Southmont would later testify that Rogers's intoxicated condition may have played a part in the tragedy: "'He [Rogers] was pretty drunk,' said the officer, and a small jar with whiskey in it was found near the guard rail of the bridge"

After hearing from additional witnesses, Judge Pickard ordered Rogers be held on a $2,000 bond with his case set for trial in superior court. Rogers would not be on trial for murder; rather, he would face the charge of manslaughter.

When Harrison Rogers faced a jury of his peers in superior court in early February, the case took an interesting turn. Judge Julius Rousseau Sr. (whose son Judge Julius Rousseau Jr. later served as a superior court judge as well), after hearing the evidence, instructed the jury to find the defendant guilty of voluntary manslaughter, involuntary manslaughter or simple assault; in the alternative, they could find him not guilty of any charge. In a case involving a homicide, the ability to convict Rogers of simple assault was unusual but was permitted only because there was no evidence he had used a deadly weapon. Nevertheless, after the jury deliberated for over an hour, they indeed found Rogers guilty of simple assault. Judge Rousseau sentenced Rogers to thirty days in jail, with his time spent working on the roads. He would later face charges for "being drunk on a highway in this county on Jan. 12, possessing and transporting liquor, and operating an automobile while under the influence of liquor."

In 1946, Annie Rogers filed for divorce against her husband. She alleged the reason for divorce was his incarceration in the state penitentiary in Trenton, New Jersey, though his crime is unknown. Harrison Rogers eventually returned to his birthplace, Buncombe County, North Carolina, and worked in a textile plant. He died in Asheville in 1964.

Vallie Michael, the bereaved wife of Ernest Michael, never remarried after her husband's death. She supported their many children by working in the Wennonah Cotton Mills in Lexington for thirty-eight years. In 1997, at the age of ninety-four, she died and was buried beside her husband at Shiloh Methodist Church.

CONCLUSION

The dedication of a library is in itself an act of faith. To bring together the records of the past and to house them in buildings where they will be preserved for the use of men and women in the future, a Nation must believe in three things. It must believe in the past. It must believe in the future. It must, above all, believe in the capacity of its own people so to learn from the past that they can gain in judgment in creating their own future.
—President Franklin D. Roosevelt, at the dedication of his library

Throughout my research and writing of this work, the holy words "blessed are the peacemakers: for they shall be called the children of God" continually resonated in my mind. They resonated because the twelve stories that have graced these pages are ones that in no way resemble peace. Rather, they are examples of men choosing violence over peacemaking through two centuries of Davidson County history. Whether these crimes were carried out by a fence post, knife or gun, their stories prove that some will do whatever it takes to inflict harm or, in some cases, survive.

Today, the various parties involved in these stories have long since passed. The crimes they committed—allegedly, in some cases—are long forgotten aside from these pages. And the adage "time heals all wounds" seems to apply. Yet the bitter tears shed long ago by each family represented in these stories are painful to reflect on. I think of the many wives left husbandless, all the children left fatherless and the bereaved mothers who were forced to bury their sons. Indeed, these men would have been blessed had they only chosen peace.

A cartoonish bailiff oversees the old courtroom at the Davidson County Historical Museum. *Author's collection.*

The upstairs courtroom in the 1858 Davidson County Courthouse is set up much the same as it was long ago. *Author's collection.*

It can be our hope that the pain of the past—from even a century ago—may be a lesson to us in our present time. As prosecutor E.J. Justice said during his closing argument at the trial of Clay Grubb, "Obe Davis has gone before a tribunal where no lawyers are needed, where another judge sits in judgment, and you, Clay Grubb, and myself will have to appear for ourselves."

While taking these stories as reminders that our history—good or bad—offers lessons for our present time, I encourage you to continue learning about our community. Spend some time at the historic 1858 Davidson County Courthouse on Main Street in Lexington, now the Davidson County Historical Museum, and walk the same halls as many of those you have read about. Stop by a Davidson County public library, where you will find records and research materials have been maintained for future generations. Walk through one of our many cemeteries and peruse the names and dates—imagine the lives of those who rest there. But no matter how you connect with history, do not fail to take to heart the lessons it can teach us. When reflecting on these lessons, you may think about the biblical command of "love your neighbor as yourself." Maybe in doing so, we may strive to live in peace, to be valuable members of society and to continue to make Davidson County a place far different than it was long ago.

BIBLIOGRAPHY

In addition to the sources listed in this bibliography, various census, marriage, death and estate records were utilized through familysearch.org. Furthermore, findagrave.com was an invaluable resource regarding burial information.

Introduction

Dispatch. "Ford Trial In Progress." August 6, 1913.
Greensboro Patriot. "Local News." August 14, 1895.
Leonard, Jacob. *Centennial History of Davidson County, North Carolina*. Raleigh, NC: Edwards & Broughton Company, 1927.
News & Observer. "Shemwell on Trial." July 2, 1895.

1. Neighbors Killing One Another

Arthur, John Preston. *Western North Carolina: A History (1730–1913)*. Asheville, NC: Edward Buncombe Chapter of the Daughters of the American Revolution, 1914.
Black, David R. *The Physical Development of the Davidson County Courthouse*. N.p., 1987.
Butler, Lindley S. "Settle, Thomas, Jr." NCpedia. https://www.ncpedia.org/biography/settle-thomas-jr.
Carolina Watchman. May 29, 1873.
———. "Murder in Davidson County." October 10, 1872.
Charlotte Democrat. April 25, 1871.
Dispatch. "100-Year-Old Stoner Home and Farm Purchased by Henry Link." December 11, 1964.

Hargrove, Tazewell. *North Carolina Reports Cases Argued and Determined in the Supreme Court of North Carolina*. Vol. 68. Raleigh, NC: Stone & Uzzell, 1873.
———. *North Carolina Reports Cases Argued and Determined in the Supreme Court of North Carolina*. Vol. 69. Raleigh, NC: Stone & Uzzell, 1873.
Heritage of Davidson County. Lexington, NC: Genealogical Society of Davidson County, 1982.
Maynard, Suzy. "Bailey, William Henry." NCpedia. https://www.ncpedia.org/biography/bailey-william-henry.
Sink, M. Jewell. "Leach, James Madison Brown." NCpedia. https://www.ncpedia.org/biography/leach-james-madison-brown.
Tri-Weekly Era. November 15, 1872.
———. "Letter from Davidson—Murder Trial." November 11, 1872.

2. A Bullet for His Brother-in-Law

Carolina Watchman. May 8, 1879.
Charlotte Democrat. "Davidson Superior Court." May 16, 1879.
Dispatch. April 17, 1901.
Salisbury Daily Truth-Index. "Mr. Barber Moves." August 30, 1900.
Union Republican. "A Sad Homicide." March 20, 1879.
WCNC staff. "Senate Agrees to Posthumous Pardon for NC Governor." WCNC Charlotte. https://www.wcnc.com/article/news/politics/senate-agrees-to-posthumous-pardon-for-nc-governor/275-374107832.
Western Sentinel. "Davidson County Tragedy." March 20, 1879.
Winston Leader. "Acquitted." May 20, 1879.

3. No Justice for Mrs. Springs

Carolina Watchman. "Davie News." November 19, 1891.
Davidson County News. "Murdered." June 24, 1897.
Dispatch. "$400 Reward." June 30, 1897.
———. "The Funeral of Mrs. A.A. Springs." June 30, 1897.
———. "Horrible Murder." June 23, 1897.
———. "A Man Captured at Mt. Airy." July 14, 1897.
———. "No Clue." June 30, 1897.
———. "Old 'March House' Was Famous for Its Good Food." April 16, 1953.
———. "The Wrong Man." July 21, 1897.
Goldsboro Daily Argus. "Burlington News." July 17, 1895.
News & Observer. "He Murdered Her." June 24, 1897.
Western Sentinel. "A Pair of Blood-Hounds." January 10, 1895.

4. Sunday's Service Leads to a Shootout

Carraway, Gertrude S. "Bryan, Henry Ravenscroft." NCpedia. https://www.ncpedia.org/biography/bryan-henry-ravenscroft.

Charlotte Daily Observer. "Conspired to Kill Grubb." May 30, 1905.

———. "The Evidence Concluded." May 18, 1905.

———. "Grubb Takes the Stand." May 17, 1905.

———. "The State Rests Its Case." May 14, 1905.

Dispatch. "Clay Grubb Killed O.L. Davis." October 19, 1904.

———. "Crump Captured by Two Mountain Boys." May 31, 1905.

———. "Crump Gets 8 Years." August 23, 1905.

———. "Democracy Forever." November 5, 1902.

———. "Down with Lawlessness." March 8, 1905.

———. "Dr. Clay Grubb Dies of Pistol Wound at Home." February 13, 1936.

———. "Evidence of the State." November 23, 1904.

———. "The Grubb Murder Trial." May 17, 1905.

———. "H. Clay Grubb Shot and Killed by His Wife." August 13, 1913.

———. "House and Barn Burned." September 5, 1900.

———. "Jubilee Items." January 25, 1894.

———. "Moved to Salisbury." March 8, 1905.

———. "Obe Davis Outlawed." October 21, 1896.

———. "Obe Davis Surrenders." November 25, 1896.

———. "State Asks for Removal." March 1, 1905.

Eagles, Brenda Marks. "Overman, Lee Slater." NCpedia. https://www.ncpedia.org/biography/overman-lee-slater.

Greene, Hugh E., and Vernelle S. Greene. *Reflections: Churchland Baptist Church, Churchland, NC.* N.p., 1987.

Hamilton, Kay M. "Hammer, William Cicero." NCpedia. https://www.ncpedia.org/biography/hammer-william-cicero.

Kickler, Dr. Troy L. "John W. Ellis." North Carolina History Project. https://northcarolinahistory.org/encyclopedia/john-w-ellis-1820-1861/.

National Register of Historic Places Inventory. Nomination form. "Community Building." 1970.

News & Observer. "In Jury's Hands." May 20, 1905.

Salisbury Evening Post. "All Evidence In." May 18, 1905.

———. "Nearing Close." May 17, 1905.

———. "A Throng Attended the Funeral and Burial of H. Clay Grubb." August 11, 1913.

Salisbury Evening Sun. "Examination of Witnesses." May 12, 1905.

———. "Proceedings of the Court Slow." May 13, 1905.

Salisbury Globe. "Grubb Now a Free Man." May 24, 1905.

State Archives of North Carolina. "Davidson County Criminal Action Papers for Henry Clay Grubb." 1904.

Union Republican. "No Bail for Grubb." November 10, 1904.

Walser, Richard. "Walser, Zeb Vance." NCpedia. https://www.ncpedia.org/biography/walser-zeb-vance.

5. Preventing an Assassination

Carolina Watchman. "Lexington and Davidson County." March 11, 1908.

Dispatch. "Danville Liquor Out." March 13, 1907.

———. "Davis Bound Over." November 28, 1906.

———. "Homicide in Hampton." November 21, 1906.

———. "John H. Moyer, Former Mayor of Lexington, Dies." September 24, 1928.

———. "Judge Moore Here." March 6, 1907.

Hill, Michael. "Moore, Daniel Killian." NCpedia. https://www.ncpedia.org/moore-dan-killian-research-branch.

6. Slayer Pays with His Life

Dispatch. "Barnhardt Is Acquitted." February 14, 1906.

———. "Bloody Tragedy Near Thomasville." February 7, 1906.

———. "Chas. F. Lookabill Killed." March 30, 1910.

———. "Squire Keen Dies Suddenly." September 22, 1909.

7. Failed to Make a Case

Dispatch. December 11, 1912.

———. February 5, 1913.

———. "Defendant's Discharged." February 12, 1913.

———. "Governor Offers Rewards for Fugitives." January 8, 1913.

———. "Rassie Butler Dead." November 27, 1912.

———. "Reward!" December 4, 1912.

Greensboro Daily Record. "Rassie Butler's Wounds Prove Fatal." November 26, 1912.

8. Shot Down in Cold Blood

Dispatch. July 23, 1913.

———. "Around Court Square." February 15, 1951.

———. "E.E. Raper's Lifetime Quest." April 3, 1976.

———. "Ford to Pen." November 26, 1913.

———. "Ford Trial in Progress." August 6, 1913.

———. "Funeral of Melvin Garland." February 21, 1921.

———. "Lee Ford Carried to Raleigh." November 26, 1913.

———. "Lee Ford in Court." April 16, 1913.

————. "Lee Ford Is Sane—So Says the Jury." August 13, 1913.

————. "Mary Elizabeth Ford." August 5, 2004.

————. "Melvin Garland Dies of Injury." February 17, 1921.

————. "Policeman Garland Killed." April 9, 1913.

————. "Robert Lee Ford." May 30, 1996.

Greensboro Daily News. "Policeman Garland of Lexington Slain by Man Named Ford." April 5, 1913.

News & Record. "Lexington: Built on Mill Power Textile Industry Transformed Town." September 22, 1990.

9. Wife's Lover Finds Demise

Dispatch. "Around Court Square." October 29, 1951.

————. "Body Taken in Arkansas." March 27, 1918.

————. "Editor Witherspoon." April 23, 1973.

————. "Graham Hege Found Guilty." June 12, 1918.

————. "Hege Fails to Secure Bail." April 3, 1918.

————. "Hege Pleads Self Defense After His Home Wrecked." June 5, 1918.

————. "Hege Preliminary Be Held Saturday." March 27, 1918.

————. "Hege Refused Pardon." January 1, 1919.

————. "J. Frank Deaderick Killed by J.G. Hege." March 20, 1918.

————. "Long-Time *Dispatch* Editor Dies." April 21, 1973.

————. "Lowe Gets Three Years." July 29, 1914.

————. "New Upholstering Plant." February 16, 1916.

————. "Opening of New Bank." March 6, 1907.

————. "Trial of Graham Hege Set to Begin Monday." May 29, 1918.

Greensboro Daily News. "Graham Hege Pleads Self-Defense on Trial for Murder of Deaderick; He Tells a Story of Wrecked Home." June 4, 1918.

————. "Hege, Slayer of Deaderick Convicted of Manslaughter." June 7, 1918.

————. "Mrs. Graham Hege on the Witness Stand Gives Husband Her Support." June 5, 1918.

————. "Preliminary Hearing Given J. Graham Hege." March 31, 1918.

High Point Enterprise. "J. Graham Hege Smiles During Selection of Jury to Try Him for Murder." June 3, 1918.

Knox News. "Former Knoxville Mayor Heiskell Never Backed Down from a Fight," December 23, 2011. https://archive.knoxnews.com/news/local/former-knoxville-mayor-heiskell-never-backed-down-from-a-fight-ep-402132640-357313541.html/.

Magruder, Nathaniel F. "Bickett, Thomas Walter." NCpedia. https://www.ncpedia.org/biography/brooks-aubrey-lee.

Robinson, Blackwell P. "Brooks, Aubrey Lee." NCpedia. https://www.ncpedia.org/biography/brooks-aubrey-lee.

State Archives of North Carolina. "Davidson County Criminal Action Papers for J. Graham Hege." 1918.

———. "Davidson County Superior Court Minutes." 1918.

State Journal. "Moral Turpitude of the 'Unwritten Law.'" June 14, 1918.

Union Republican. "Lexington Dispatch." January 16, 1919.

Winston-Salem Journal. "Self Defense Is the Plea Offered by J. Graham Hege." June 4, 1918.

10. Struck Without Warning

Daily Telegram. "News Lawyers." October 13, 1915.

Dispatch. "$400 Reward Offered for Capture of Garwood Slayer; Accomplice Is in Jail," August 11, 1924.

———. "Garwood Slayers May Be Arraigned Here in Afternoon." August 18, 1924.

———. "Governor Again Shows Favor to Hale and Leake." November 10, 1924.

———. "Governor Gives Garwood Slayers Month's Respite." October 6, 1924.

———. "Governor Won't Change Sentence of Kenneth Hale." December 22, 1924.

———. "Kenneth Hale to Seek Commutation to Life Sentence." September 22, 1924.

———. "Lawyers Start Arguments." August 22, 1924.

———. "Leake and Hale Given Death Sentence." August 23, 1924.

———. "Memories of the Meares Family." May 3, 1985.

———. "Murderers of Garwood Confessed All." August 25, 1924.

———. "Paper Tells Condemned Men Their Execution Date." November 9, 1972.

Greensboro Daily News. "Both Leak and Hale Charge Other with Striking Blows That Killed Charlie Garwood." August 17, 1924.

———. "Charles Garwood, Lexington Taxicab Driver, Brutally Murdered Thursday Night; Two Negroes Are Being Sought." August 9, 1924.

———. "Hale and Leak to Know Their Fate Before the Setting of Sun Today." August 23, 1924.

———. "Hale Knows Spruill Will Say 'Hide 'Em.'" August 23, 1924.

———. "John Leak and Kenneth Hale Stand Up in Davidson Courthouse and Receive Sentence of Death in Electric Chair." August 24, 1924.

———. "Leak and Hale Each Enters a Plea of Being in Murder Car; Each Denies Killing Garwood." August 19, 1924.

———. "Negro Under Arrest at Charlotte Tells of Garwood Killing." August 10, 1924.

———. "Piece of Iron with Which Garwood Was Murdered Identified as Being in Possession of Leak Day Before." August 22, 1924.

———. "Spruill Begins Weaving a Strong Web of Evidence Around Leak and Hale." August 21, 1924.

Greensboro Daily Record. "Charlie Garwood, Jitney Driver, Is Beaten to Death." August 8, 1924.

———. "Leak and Hale Died in Chair; Killed Garwood." January 5, 1925.

————. "Leak Declares Hale Murdered Charlie Garwood." August 16, 1924.

————. "Part of Jury Selected for Trying Negroes." August 20, 1924.

————. "Testify Leak Is Man Who Got Iron Bar with Which Chas. Garwood Was Killed." August 21, 1924.

State Archives of North Carolina. "Davidson County Criminal Action Papers, State v. Leak and Hale." 1924.

————. "Davidson County Superior Court Minutes, Volume 25." 1924.

Twin City Sentinel. "Hale and Leak to Die October 9th." August 25, 1924.

————. "Verdict Is Expected in a Few Hours in Lexington Murder Trial." August 23, 1924.

Winston-Salem Journal. "Garwood Killing as Negroes Told It Is Given Jury." August 22, 1924.

11. Hunting Leads to Feuding

Courier. "Larthy Hedrick." July 25, 1929.

Dispatch. "Biscoe Robbery Car Abandoned in This County." February 21, 1935.

————. "John Kindley Is Cut to Death by Larthy Hedrick." March 29, 1926.

————. "Larthy Hedrick Rumors Denied by Officials Here." March 7, 1935.

————. "Twenty Years Is Sentence Given Larthy Hedrick." May 10, 1926.

Greensboro Daily News. "Arguments to Start Today, Hedrick Case." May 7, 1926.

————. "Hedrick Gets Term of 20 to 30 Years." May 9, 1926.

————. "Hedrick Is Ordered Held for Grand Jury." March 27, 1926.

————. "L.L. Hedrick Will Go On Trial for His Life." May 4, 1926.

————. "Three Eye-Witnesses Tell about Hedrick's Attack Upon Kindley." May 6, 1926.

Greensboro Record. "Deadly Weapons Harvest." May 13, 1926.

Winston-Salem Journal. "Hedrick to Offer Strong Defense." April 14, 1926.

————. "Thomasville Man Stabbed to Death; Ends an Old Feud." March 26, 1926.

12. Murder, Manslaughter or Assault

Annual of the Baptist State Convention of North Carolina. Wake Forest, NC: Baptist State Convention of North Carolina, 1972.

Carolina Watchman. "Spencer Officer Convicted of Simple Assault." February 7, 1936.

Dispatch. "Negro Prisoner Wields Knife on Police Officer." September 20, 1926.

————. "Rogers Murder Charge Is Now Manslaughter." January 20, 1936.

————. "Rogers to Face Liquor Charges in County Court." February 17, 1936.

————. "Spencer Officer Held for Killing of Ernest Michael." January 13, 1936.

————. "Vallie Y. Michael." September 17, 1997.

Holland, Irma Ragan. "Olive, Hubert Etheridge, Sr." NCpedia. https://www.ncpedia.org/biography/olive-hubert-ethridge-sr.

ABOUT THE AUTHOR

Caleb L. Sink is a lifelong resident of Davidson County, and his family settled in the area before the county's establishment. He is a graduate of Davidson-Davie Community College, where he obtained his associate's degree in paralegal technology. This is his first publication with The History Press, having previously self-published various writings about Davidson County. In addition to being a freelance writer, Caleb works in the North Carolina Judicial Branch and serves as the president of the Genealogical Society of Davidson County.